Reflections; Or Sentences and Moral Maxims

by Francois Duc De La Rochefoucauld

Translated by J. W. Willis Bund and J. Hain Friswell

Translators' Introduction

The description of the ancient regime; in France, a despotism tempered by epigrams, like most epigrammatic sentences, contains some truth, with much fiction. The society of the last half of the seventeenth, and the whole of the eighteenth centuries, was doubtless greatly influenced by the precise and terse mode in which the popular writers of that date expressed their thoughts. To a people naturally inclined to think that every possible view, every conceivable argument, upon a question is included in a short aphorism, a shrug, and the word; truths expressed in condensed sentences must always have a peculiar charm. It is, perhaps, from this love of epigram, that we find so many eminent French writers of maxims. Pascal, De Retz, La Rochefoucauld, La Bruyiee, Montesquieu, and Vau- venargues, each contributed to the rich stock of French epigrams. No other country can show such a list of brilliant writers--in England certainly we can- not. Our most celebrated, Lord Bacon, has, by his other works, so surpassed his maxims, that their fame is, to a great measure, obscured. The only Englishman who could have rivalled La Rochefou- cauld or La Bruyiee was the Earl of Chesterfield, and he only could have done so from his very inti- mate connexion with France; but unfortunately his brilliant genius was spent in the impossible task of trying to refine a boorish young Briton, in ;cutting blocks with a razor.

Of all the French epigrammatic writers La Rochefou- cauld is at once the most widely known, and the most distinguished. Voltaire, whose opinion on the cen- tury of Louis XIV. is entitled to the greatest weight, says, “One of the works that most largely contributed to form the taste of the nation, and to diffuse a spirit of justice and precision, is the collection of maxims, by Francois Duc de la Rochefoucauld.

This Francois, the second Duc de la Rochefoucauld, Prince de Marsillac, the author of the maxims, was one of the most illustrious members of the most illus- trious families among the French noblesse. Descended from the ancient Dukes of Guienne, the founder of the Family Fulk or Foucauld, a younger branch of the House of Lusignan, was at the commencement of the eleventh century the Seigneur of a small town, La Roche, in the Angounois. Our chief knowledge of this feudal lord is drawn from the monkish chronicles. As the benefactor of the various abbeys and monas- teries in his province, he is naturally spoken of by them in terms of eulogy, and in the charter of one of the abbeys of Angouleme he is called, vir nobilissimus Fulcaldus; His territorial power enabled him to adopt what was then, as is still in Scotland, a com- mon custom, to prefix the name of his estate to his surname, and thus to create and transmit to his descendants the illustrious surname of La Rochefou- cauld.

From that time until that great crisis in the history of the French aristocracy, the Revolution of 1789, the family of La Rochefoucauld have been, "if not first, in the very first line" of that most illustrious body. One Seigneur served under Philip Augustus against Richard Coeur de Lion, and was made prisoner at the battle of Gisors. The eighth Seigneur Guy performed a great tilt at Bordeaux, attended (according to Froissart) to the Lists by some two hundred of his kindred and relations. The sixteenth Seigneur Francais was cham- berlain to Charles VIII. and Louis XII., and stood at the font as sponsor, giving his name to that last light of French chivalry, Francis I. In 1515 he was created a baron, and was afterwards advanced to a count, on account of his great service to Francis and his predecessors.

The second count pushed the family fortune still further by obtaining a patent as the Prince de Mar- sillac. His widow, Anne de Polignac, entertained Charles V. at the family chateau at Verteuil, in so princely a manner that on leaving Charles observed. He had never entered a house so redolent of high virtue, uprightness, and lordliness as that mansion.

The third count, after serving with distinction under the Duke of Guise against the Spaniards, was made prisoner at St. Quintin, and only regained his liberty to fall a victim to the bloody infamy of St. Bartholomew. His son, the fourth count, saved with difficulty from that massacre, after serving with dis- tinction in the religious wars, was taken prisoner in a skirmish at St. Yriex la Perche, and murdered by the Leaguers in cold blood.

The fifth count, one of the ministers of Louis XIII., after fighting against the English and Buck- ingham at the Ile de Re was created a duke. His son Francis, the second duke, by his writings has made the family name a household word.

The third duke fought in many of the earlier campaigns of Louis XIV. at Torcy, Lille, Cambray, and was dangerously wounded at the passage of the Rhine.

From his bravery he rose to high favour at Court, and was appointed Master of the Horse (Grand Veneur) and Lord Chamberlain. His son, the fourth duke, commanded the regiment of Navarre, and took part in storming the village of Neerwinden on the day when William III. was defeated at Landen. He was afterwards created Duc de la Rochequyon and Marquis de Liancourt.

The fifth duke, banished from Court by Louis XV., became the friend of the philosopher Voltaire.

The sixth duke, the friend of Condorcet, was the last of the long line of noble lords who bore that distinguished name. In those terrible days of Sep- tember, 1792, when the French people were proclaim- ing universal humanity, the duke was seized as an aristocrat by the mob at Gisors and put to death behind his own carriage, in which sat his mother and his wife, at the very place where, some six centuries previously, his ancestor had been taken prisoner in a fair fight. A modern writer has spoken of this murder;as an admirable reprisal upon the grandson for the writings and conduct of the grandfather; But M. Sainte Beuve observes as to this, he can see nothing admirable in the death of the duke, and if it proves anything, it is only that the grandfather was not so wrong in his judgment of men as is usually supposed.

Francis, the author, was born on the 15th December 1615. M. Sainte Beuve divides his life into four periods, first, from his birth till he was thirty-five, when he became mixed up in the war of the Fronde; the second period, during the progress of that war; the third, the twelve years that followed, while he re- covered from his wounds, and wrote his maxims dur- ing his retirement from society; and the last from that time till his death.

In the same way that Herodotus calls each book of his history by the name of one of the muses, so each of these four periods of La Rochefoucauld's life may be associated with the name of a woman who was for the time his ruling passion. These four ladies are the Duchesse de Chevreuse, the Duchesse de Longueville, Madame de Sable and Madame de La Fayette.

La Rochefoucauld's early education was neglected; his father, occupied in the affairs of state, either had not, or did not devote any time to his education. His natural talents and his habits of observation soon, however, supplied all deficiencies. By birth and sta- tion placed in the best society of the French Court, he soon became a most finished courtier. Knowing how precarious Court favour then was, his father, when young Rochefoucauld was only nine years old, sent him into the army. He was subsequently at- tached to the regiment of Auvergne. Though but sixteen he was present, and took part in the mili- tary operations at the siege of Cassel. The Court of Louis XIII. was then ruled imperiously by Richelieu. The Duke de la Rochefoucauld was strongly opposed to the Cardinal's party. By joining in the plots of Gaston of Orleans, he gave Richelieu an opportunity of ridding Paris of his opposition. When those plots were discovered, the Duke was sent into a sort of banishment to Blois. His son, who was then at Court with him, was, upon the pretext of a liaison with Mdlle. d'Hautefort, one of the ladies in waiting on the Queen (Anne of Austria), but in reality to pre- vent the Duke learning what was passing at Paris, sent with his father. The result of the exile was Roche- foucauld's marriage. With the exception that his wife's name was Mdlle. Vivonne, and that she was the mother of five sons and three daughters, nothing is known of her. While Rochefoucauld and his father were at Blois, the Duchesse de Chevreuse, one of the beauties of the Court, and the mistress of Louis, was banished to Tours. She and Rochefou- cauld met, and soon became intimate, and for a time she was destined to be the one motive of his actions. The Duchesse was engaged in a correspondence with the Court of Spain and the Queen. Into this plot Rochefoucauld threw himself with all his energy; his connexion with the Queen brought him back to his old love Mdlle. d'Hautefort, and led him to her party, which he afterwards followed. The course he took shut him off from all chance of Court favour. The King regarded him with coldness, the Cardinal with irritation. Although the Bastile and the scaffold, the fate of Chalais and Montmorency, were before his eyes, they failed to deter him from plotting. He was about twenty-three; returning to Paris, he warmly sided with the Queen. He says in his Memoirs that the only persons she could then trust were him- self and Mdlle. d'Hautefort, and it was proposed he should take both of them from Paris to Brussels. Into this plan he entered with all his youthful indiscretion, it being for several reasons the very one he would wish to adopt, as it would strengthen his influence with Anne of Austria, place Richelieu and his master in an uncomfortable position, and save Mdlle. d'Hautefort from the attentions the King was showing her.

But Richelieu of course discovered this plot, and Rochefoucauld was, of course, sent to the Bastile. He was liberated after a week's imprisonment, but banished to his chateau at Verteuil.

The reason for this clemency was that the Cardinal desired to win Rochefoucauld from the Queen's party. A command in the army was offered to him, but by the Queen's orders refused.

For some three years Rochefoucauld remained at Verteuil, waiting the time for his reckoning with Richelieu; speculating on the King's death, and the favours he would then receive from the Queen. During this period he was more or less engaged in plotting against his enemy the Cardinal, and hatching treason with Cinq Mars and De Thou.

M. Sainte Beuve says, that unless we study this first part of Rochefoucauld's life, we shall never under- stand his maxims. The bitter disappointment of the passionate love, the high hopes then formed, the deceit and treachery then witnessed, furnished the real key to their meaning. The cutting cynicism of the morality was built on the ruins of that chivalrous ambition and romantic affection. He saw his friend Cinq Mars sent to the scaffold, himself betrayed by men whom he had trusted, and the only reason he could assign for these actions was intense selfishness.

Meanwhile, Richelieu died. Rochefoucauld re- turned to Court, and found Anne of Austria regent, and Mazarin minister. The Queen's former friends flocked there in numbers, expecting that now their time of prosperity had come. They were bitterly dis- appointed. Mazarin relied on hope instead of grati- tude, to keep the Queen's adherents on his side. The most that any received were promises that were never performed. In after years, doubtless, Rochefoucauld's recollection of his disappointment led him to write the maxim: We promise according to our hopes, we per- form according to our fears. But he was not even to receive promises; he asked for the Governorship of Havre, which was then vacant. He was flatly refused. Disappointment gave rise to anger, and uniting with his old flame, the Duchesse de Chevreuse, who had received the same treatment, and with the Duke of Beaufort, they formed a conspiracy against the govern- ment. The plot was, of course, discovered and crushed. Beaufort was arrested, the Duchesse banished. Irri- tated and disgusted, Rochefoucauld went with the Duc d'Enghein, who was then joining the army, on a campaign, and here he found the one love of his life, the Duke's sister, Mdme. de Longueville. This lady, young, beautiful, and accomplished, obtained a great ascendancy over Rochefoucauld, and was the cause of his taking the side of Cond?in the subsequent civil war. Rochefoucauld did not stay long with the army. He was badly wounded at the siege of Mardik, and returned from thence to Paris. On recovering from his wounds, the war of the Fronde broke out. This war is said to have been most ridiculous, as being carried on without a definite object, a plan, or a leader. But this description is hardly correct; it was the struggle of the French nobility against the rule of the Court; an attempt, the final attempt, to re- cover their lost influence over the state, and to save themselves from sinking under the rule of cardinals and priests.

With the general history of that war we have nothing to do; it is far too complicated and too confused to be stated here. The memoirs of Roche-foucauld and De Retz will give the details to those who desire to trace the contests of the factions--the course of the intrigues. We may confine ourselves to its progress so far as it relates to the Duc de la Roche- foucauld.

On the Cardinal causing the Princes de Cond?and Conti, and the Duc de Longueville, to be arrested, Rochefoucauld and the Duchess fled into Normandy. Leaving her at Dieppe, he went into Poitou, of which province he had some years pre- viously bought the post of governor. He was there joined by the Duc de Bouillon, and he and the Duke marched to, and occupied Bordeaux. Cardinal Ma- zarin and Marechal de la Meilleraie advanced in force on Bordeaux, and attacked the town. A bloody battle followed. Rochefoucauld defended the town with the greatest bravery, and repulsed the Cardinal. Notwithstanding the repulse, the burghers of Bor- deaux were anxious to make peace, and save the city from destruction. The Parliament of Bordeaux com- pelled Rochefoucauld to surrender. He did so, and returned nominally to Poitou, but in reality in secret to Paris.

There he found the Queen engaged in trying to maintain her position by playing off the rival parties of the Prince Cond?and the Cardinal De Retz against each other. Rochefoucauld eagerly espoused his old party--that of Cond? In August, 1651, the contend- ing parties met in the Hall of the Parliament of Paris, and it was with great difficulty they were prevented from coming to blows even there. It is even said that Rochefoucauld had ordered his followers to murder De Retz.

Rochefoucauld was soon to undergo a bitter disap- pointment. While occupied with party strife and faction in Paris, Madame de Chevreuse left him, and formed an alliance with the Duc de Nemours. Rochefoucauld still loved her. It was, probably, thinking of this that he afterwards wrote, “Jealousy is born with love, but does not die with it; He endea- voured to get Madame de Chatillon, the old mistress of the Duc de Nemours, reinstated in favour, but in this he did not succeed. The Duc de Nemours was soon after killed in a duel. The war went on, and after several indecisive skirmishes, the decisive battle was fought at Paris, in the Faubourg St. Antoine, where the Parisians first learnt the use or the abuse of their favourite defence, the barricade. In this battle, Rochefoucauld behaved with great bravery. He was wounded in the head, a wound which for a time deprived him of his sight. Before he recovered, the war was over, Louis XIV. had attained his ma- jority, the gold of Mazarin, the arms of Turenne, had been successful, the French nobility were vanquished, the court supremacy established.

This completed Rochefoucauld's active life.

When he recovered his health, he devoted himself to society. Madame assumed a hold over him. He lived a quiet life, and occupied himself in composing an account of his early life, called his Memoirs and his immortal Maxims

From the time he ceased to take part in public life, Rochefoucauld's real glory began. Having acted the various parts of soldier, politician, and lover with but small success, he now commenced the part of moralist, by which he is known to the world.

Living in the most brilliant society that France possessed, famous from his writings, distinguished from the part he had taken in public affairs, he formed the centre of one of those remarkable French literary societies, a society which numbered among its members La Fontaine, Racine, Boileau. Among his most attached friends was Madame de La Fayette, and this friend- ship continued until his death. He was not, however, destined to pass away in that gay society without some troubles. At the passage of the Rhine in 1672 two of his sons were engaged; the one was killed, the other severely wounded.

Rochefoucauld was much affected by this, but perhaps still more by the death of the young Duc de Longueville, who perished on the same occasion.

Sainte Beuve says that the cynical book and that young life were the only fruits of the war of the Fronde. Madame de Savigne who was with him when he heard the news of the death of so much that was dear to him, says, "I saw his heart laid bare on that cruel occasion, and his courage, his merit, his tender- ness, and good sense surpassed all I ever met with. I hold his wit and accomplishments as nothing in com- parison. The combined effect of his wounds and the gout caused the last years of Rochefoucauld's life to be spent in great pain. Madame de Savigne who was {with} him continually during his last illness, speaks of the fortitude with which he bore his sufferings as something to be admired. Writing to her daughter, she says, "Believe me, it is not for nothing he has moralised all his life; he has thought so often on his last moments that they are nothing new or unfamiliar to him.

In his last illness, the great moralist was attended by the great divine, Bossuet. Whether that match- less eloquence or his own philosophic calm had, in spite of his writings, brought him into the state Madame de Savigne describes, we know not; but one, or both, contributed to his passing away in a manner that did not disgrace a French noble or a French philosopher. On the 11th March, 1680, he ended his stormy life in peace after so much strife, a loyal subject after so much treason.

Rochefoucauld left behind him only two works, the one, Memoirs of his own time, the other the Maxims. The first described the scenes in which his youth had been spent, and though written in a lively style, and giving faithful pictures of the intrigues and the scandals of the court during Louis XIV.'s minority, yet, except to the historian, has ceased at the present day to be of much interest. It forms, perhaps, the true key to understand the special as opposed to general application of the maxims.

Notwithstanding the assertion of Bayle, that there are few people so bigoted to antiquity as not to prefer the Memoirs of La Rochefoucauld to the Commen- taries of Caesar; or the statement of Voltaire, "that the Memoirs are universally read and the Maxims are learnt by heart; few persons at the present day ever heard of the Memoirs, and the knowledge of most as to the Maxims is confined to that most celebrated of all, though omitted from his last edition, “There is something in the misfortunes of our best friends which does not wholly displease us.; Yet it is difficult to assign a cause for this; no book is perhaps oftener unwittingly quoted, none certainly oftener unblushingly pillaged; upon none have so many contradictory opinions been given.

Few books, says Mr. Hallam, have been more highly extolled, or more severely blamed, than the maxims of the Duke of Rochefoucauld, and that not only here, but also in France.; Rousseau speaks of it as, a sad and melancholy book; though he goes on to say it is usually so in youth when we do not like seeing man as he; Voltaire says of it, in the words above quoted, One of the works which most contri- buted to form the taste of the (French) nation, and to give it a spirit of justness and precision, was the collection of the maxims of Francois Duc de la Roche- foucauld, though there is scarcely more than one truth running through the book--that;self-love is the motive of everything;--yet this thought is presented under so many varied aspects that it is nearly always striking. It is not so much a book as it is materials for ornamenting a book. This little collection was read with avidity, it taught people to think, and to comprise their thoughts in a lively, precise, and delicate turn of expression. This was a merit which, before him, no one in Europe had attained since the revival of letters;

Dr. Johnson speaks of it as ;the only book written by a man of fashion, of which professed authors need be jealous.;

Lord Chesterfield, in his letters to his son, says, Till you come to know mankind by your experience, I know no thing nor no man that can in the mean- time bring you so well acquainted with them as Le Duc de la Rochefoucauld. His little book of maxims, which I would advise you to look into for some moments at least every day of your life, is, I fear, too like and too exact a picture of human nature. I own it seems to degrade it, but yet my experience does not convince me that it degrades it unjustly.

Bishop Butler, on the other hand, blames the book in no measured terms. There is a strange affecta- tion, says the bishop, “in some people of explaining away all particular affection, and representing the whole life as nothing but one continued exercise of self-love. Hence arise that surprising confusion and perplexity in the Epicureans of old, Hobbes, the author of 'Reflexions Morales,' and the whole set of writers, of calling actions interested which are done of the most manifest known interest, merely for the gratification of a present passion.

The judgment the reader will be most inclined to adopt will perhaps be either that of Mr. Hallam, Con- cise and energetic in expression, reduced to those short aphorisms which leave much to the reader's acuteness and yet save his labour, not often obscure, and never wearisome, an evident generalisation of long experience, without pedantry, without method, without deductive reasonings, yet wearing an appear- ance at least of profundity; they delight the intelli- gent though indolent man of the world, and must be read with some admiration by the philosopher . . . . yet they bear witness to the contracted observation and the precipitate inferences which an intercourse with a single class of society scarcely fails to generate.” Or that of Addison, who speaks of Rochefoucauld “as the great philosopher for administering consola- tion to the idle, the curious, and the worthless part of mankind.”

We are fortunately in possession of materials such as rarely exist to enable us to form a judgment of Rochefoucauld's character. We have, with a vanity that could only exist in a Frenchman, a description or portrait of himself, of his own painting, and one of those inimitable living sketches in which his great enemy, Cardinal De Retz, makes all the chief actors in the court of the regency of Anne of Austria pass across the stage before us.

We will first look on the portrait Rochefoucauld has left us of himself;I am, says he, of a medium height, active, and well-proportioned. My complexion dark, but uniform, a high forehead; and of moderate height, black eyes, small, deep set, eyebrows black and thick but well placed. I am rather embarrassed in talking of my nose, for it is neither flat nor aquiline, nor large; nor pointed: but I believe, as far as I can say, it is too large than too small, and comes down just a trifle too low. I have a large mouth, lips generally red enough, neither shaped well nor badly. I have white teeth, and fairly even. I have been told I have a little too much chin. I have just looked at myself in the glass to ascertain the fact, and I do not know how to decide. As to the shape of my face, it is either square or oval, but which I should find it very diffi- cult to say. I have black hair, which curls by nature, and thick and long enough to entitle me to lay claim to a fine head. I have in my countenance somewhat of grief and pride, which gives many people an idea I despise them, although I am not at all given to do so. My gestures are very free, rather inclined to be too much so, for in speaking they make me use too much action. Such, candidly, I believe I am in out- ward appearance, and I believe it will be found that what I have said above of myself is not far from the real case. I shall use the same truthfulness in the remainder of my picture, for I have studied my- self sufficiently to know myself well; and I will lack neither boldness to speak as freely as I can of my good qualities, nor sincerity to freely avow that I have faults.

In the first place, to speak of my temper. I am melancholy, and I have hardly been seen for the last three or four years to laugh above three or four times. It seems to me that my melancholy would be even endurable and pleasant if I had none but what be- longed to me constitutionally; but it arises from so many other causes, fills my imagination in such a way, and possesses my mind so strongly that for the greater part of my time I remain without speaking a word, or give no meaning to what I say. I am ex- tremely reserved to those I do not know, and I am not very open with the greater part of those I do. It is a fault I know well, and I should neglect no means to correct myself of it; but as a certain gloomy air I have tends to make me seem more reserved than I am in fact, and as it is not in our power to rid ourselves of a bad expression that arises from a natu- ral conformation of features, I think that even when I have cured myself internally, externally some bad expression will always remain.

I have ability. I have no hesitation in saying it, as for what purpose should I pretend otherwise. So great circumvention, and so great depreciation, in speaking of the gifts one has, seems to me to hide a little vanity under an apparent modesty, and craftily to try to make others believe in greater virtues than are imputed to us. On my part I am content not to be considered better-looking than I am, nor of a bet- ter temper than I describe, nor more witty and clever than I am. Once more, I have ability, but a mind spoilt by melancholy, for though I know my own language tolerably well, and have a good memory, a mode of thought not particularly confused, I yet have so great a mixture of discontent that I often say what I have to say very badly.

The conversation of gentlemen is one of the plea- sures that most amuses me. I like it to be serious and morality to form the substance of it. Yet I also know how to enjoy it when trifling; and if I do not make many witty speeches, it is not because I do not appreciate the value of trifles well said, and that I do not find great amusement in that manner of rail- lery in which certain prompt and ready-witted per- sons excel so well. I write well in prose; I do well in verse; and if I was envious of the glory that springs from that quarter, I think with a little labour I could acquire some reputation. I like reading, in general; but that in which one finds something to polish the wit and strengthen the soul is what I like best. But, above all, I have the greatest pleasure in reading with an intelligent person, for then we reflect constantly upon what we read, and the observations we make form the most pleasant and useful form of conversation there is.

I am a fair critic of the works in verse and prose that are shown me; but perhaps I speak my opinion with almost too great freedom. Another fault in me is that I have sometimes a spirit of delicacy far too scrupulous, and a spirit of criticism far too severe. I do not dislike an argument, and I often of my own free will engage in one; but I generally back my opinion with too much warmth, and sometimes, when the wrong side is advocated against me, from the strength of my zeal for reason, I become a little un- reasonable myself.

I have virtuous sentiments, good inclinations, and so strong a desire to be a wholly good man that my friend cannot afford me a greater pleasure than can- didly to show me my faults. Those who know me most intimately, and those who have the goodness sometimes to give me the above advice, know that I always receive it with all the joy that could be ex- pected, and with all reverence of mind that could be desired.

I have all the passions pretty mildly, and pretty well under control. I am hardly ever seen in a rage, and I never hated any one. I am not, however, in- capable of avenging myself if I have been offended, or if my honour demanded I should resent an insult put upon me; on the contrary, I feel clear that duty would so well discharge the office of hatred in me that I should follow my revenge with even greater keenness than other people.

Ambition does not weary me. I fear but few things, and I do not fear death in the least. I am but little given to pity, and I could wish I was not so at all. Though there is nothing I would not do to com- fort an afflicted person, and I really believe that one should do all one can to show great sympathy to him for his misfortune, for miserable people are so foolish that this does them the greatest good in the world; yet I also hold that we should be content with expressing sympathy, and carefully avoid having any. It is a passion that is wholly worthless in a well-regu- lated mind, which only serves to weaken the heart, and which should be left to ordinary persons, who, as they never do anything from reason, have need of passions to stimulate their actions.

I love my friends; and I love them to such an extent that I would not for a moment weigh my interest against theirs. I condescend to them, I patiently endure their bad temper. But, also, I do not make much of their caresses, and I do not feel great uneasiness in their absence.

Naturally, I have but little curiosity about the majority of things that stir up curiosity in other men. I am very secret, and I have less difficulty than most men in holding my tongue as to what is told me in confidence. I am most particular as to my word, and I would never fail, whatever might be the conse- quence, to do what I had promised; and I have made this an inflexible law during the whole of my life.

I keep the most punctilious civility to women. I do not believe I have ever said anything before them which could cause them annoyance. When their intellect is cultivated, I prefer their society to that of men: one there finds a mildness one does not meet with among ourselves, and it seems to me beyond this that they express themselves with more neatness, and give a more agreeable turn to the things they talk about. As for flirtation, I formerly indulged in a little, now I shall do so no more, though I am still young. I have renounced all flirtation, and I am simply astonished that there are still so many sensible people who can occupy their time with it.

I wholly approve of real loves; they indicate great- ness of soul, and although, in the uneasiness they give rise to, there is a something contrary to strict wisdom, they fit in so well with the most severe virtue, that I believe they cannot be censured with justice. To me who have known all that is fine and grand in the lofty aspirations of love, if I ever fall in love, it will as- suredly be in love of that nature. But in accordance with the present turn of my mind, I do not believe that the knowledge I have of it will ever change from my mind to my heart.”

Such is his own description of himself. Let us now turn to the other picture, delineated by the man who was his bitterest enemy, and whom (we say it with regret) Rochefoucauld tried to murder.

Cardinal De Retz thus paints him:--In M. de la Rochefoucauld there was ever an indescribable something. From his infancy he always wanted to be mixed up with plots, at a time when he could not understand even the smallest interests (which has indeed never been his weak point,) or comprehend greater ones, which in another sense has never been his strong point. He was never fitted for any matter, and I really cannot tell the reason. His glance was not sufficiently wide, and he could not take in at once all that lay in his sight, but his good sense, perfect in theories, combined with his gentleness, his winning ways, his pleasing manners, which are perfect, should more than compensate for his lack of penetration. He always had a natural irresoluteness, but I cannot say to what this irresolution is to be attributed. It could not arise in him from the wealth of his imagina- tion, for that was anything but lively. I cannot put it down to the barrenness of his judgment, for, although he was not prompt in action, he had a good store of reason. We see the effects of this irresolution, although we cannot assign a cause for it. He was never a general, though a great soldier; never, na- turally, a good courtier, although he had always a good idea of being so. He was never a good partizan, although all his life engaged in intrigues. That air of pride and timidity which your see in his private life, is turned in business into an apologetic manner. He always believed he had need of it; and this, com- bined with his 'Maxims,' which show little faith in virtue, and his habitual custom, to give up matters with the same haste he undertook them, leads me to the conclusion that he would have done far better to have known his own mind, and have passed himself off, as he could have done, for the most polished courtier, the most agreeable man in private life that had appeared in his century.

It is but justice to the Cardinal to say, that the Duc is not painted in such dark colours as we should have expected, judging from what we know of the character of De Retz. With his marvellous power of depicting character, a power unrivalled, except by St. Simon and perhaps by Lord Clarendon, we should have expected the malignity of the priest would have stamped the features of his great enemy with the impress of infamy, and not have simply made him appear a courtier, weak, insincere, and nothing more. Though rather beyond our subject, the character of Cardinal de Retz, as delineated by Mdme. Savigne in one of her letters, will help us to form a true conclu- sion on the different characters of the Duc and the Cardinal. She says Paul de Gondi Cardinal de Retz possesses great elevation of character, a certain extent of intellect, and more of the ostentation than of the true greatness of courage. He has an extraordinary memory, more energy than polish in his words, an easy humour, docility of character, and weakness in submitting to the complaints and reproaches of his friends, a little piety, some appearances of religion. He appears ambitious without being really so. Vanity and those who have guided him, have made him undertake great things, almost all opposed to his profession. He ex- cited the greatest troubles in the State without any design of turning them to account, and far from declaring himself the enemy of Cardinal Mazarin with any view of occupying his place, he thought of nothing but making himself an object of dread to him, and flattering himself with the false vanity of being his rival. He was clever enough, however, to take advantage of the public calamities to get himself made Cardinal. He endured his imprisonment with firmness, and owed his liberty solely to his own daring. In the obscurity of a life of wandering and concealment, his indolence for many years supported him with reputation. He preserved the Archbishopric of Paris against the power of Cardinal Mazarin, but after the death of that minister, he resigned it without knowing what he was doing, and without making use of the opportunity to promote the interests of him- self and his friends. He has taken part in several conclaves, and his conduct has always increased his reputation.

His natural bent is to indolence, nevertheless he labours with activity in pressing business, and reposes with indifference when it is concluded. He has great presence of mind, and knows so well how to turn it to his own advantage on all occasions presented him by fortune, that it would seem as if he had foreseen and desired them. He loves to narrate, and seeks to dazzle all his listeners indifferently by his extraor- dinary adventures, and his imagination often supplies him with more than his memory. The generality of his qualities are false, and what has most contributed to his reputation is his power of throwing a good light on his faults. He is insensible alike to hatred and to friendship, whatever pains he may be at to appear taken up with the one or the other. He is incapable of envy or avarice, whether from virtue or from care- lessness. He has borrowed more from his friends than a private person could ever hope to be able to repay; he has felt the vanity of acquiring so much on credit, and of undertaking to discharge it. He has neither taste nor refinement; he is amused by every- thing and pleased by nothing. He avoids difficult matters with considerable address, not allowing people to penetrate the slight acquaintance he has with every- thing. The retreat he has just made from the world is the most brilliant and the most unreal action of his life; it is a sacrifice he has made to his pride under the pretence of devotion; he quits the court to which he cannot attach himself, and retires from a world which is retiring from him.

The Maxims were first published in 1665, with a preface by Segrais. This preface was omitted in the subsequent editions. The first edition contained 316 maxims, counting the last upon death, which was not numbered. The second in 1666 contained only 102; the third in 1671, and the fourth in 1675, 413. In this last edition we first meet with the introductory maxim, “Our virtues are gene- rally but disguised vices.” The edition of 1678, the fifth, increased the number to 504. This was the last edition revised by the author, and pub- lished in his lifetime. The text of that edition has been used for the present translation. The next edition, the sixth, was published in 1693, about thirteen years after the author's death. This edition included fifty new maxims, attributed by the editor to Rochefoucauld. Most likely they were his writing, as the fact was never denied by his family, through whose permission they were published. They form the third supplement to the translation. This sixth edition was published by Claude Barbin, and the French editions since that time have been too nu- merous to be enumerated. The great popularity of the Maxims is perhaps best shown from the numerous translations that have been made of them. No less than eight English translations, or so-called transla- tions, have appeared; one American, a Swedish, and a Spanish translation, an Italian imitation, with parallel passages, and an English imitation by Hazlitt. The titles of the English editions are as follows:-- i. Seneca Unmasked. By Mrs. Aphara Behn. Lon- don, 1689. She calls the author the Duke of Rushfucave. ii. Moral Maxims and Reflections, in four parts. By the Duke de la Rochefoucauld. Now made English. London, 1694. 12 mo. iii. Moral Maxims and Reflections of the Duke de la Rochefoucauld. Newly made English. Lon- don, 1706. 12 mo. iv. Moral Maxims of the Duke de la Rochefoucauld. Translated from the French. With notes. Lon- don, 1749. 12 mo. v. Maxims and Moral Reflections of the Duke de la Rochefoucauld. Revised and improved. London, 1775. 8 vo. vi. Maxims and Moral Reflections of the Duke de la Rochefoucauld. A new edition, revised and im- proved, by L. D. London, 1781. 8 vo. vii. The Gentleman's Library. La Rochefoucauld's Maxims and Moral Reflections. London, 1813. 12 mo. viii.Moral Reflections, Sentences, and Maxims of the Duke de la Rochefoucauld, newly translated from the French; with an introduction and notes. London, 1850. 16 mo. ix. Maxims and Moral Reflections of the Duke de la Rochefoucauld: with a Memoir by the Chevalier de Chatelain. London, 1868. 12 mo.

The perusal of the Maxims will suggest to every reader to a greater or less degree, in accordance with the extent of his reading, parallel passages, and simi- lar ideas. Of ancient writers Rochefoucauld most strongly reminds us of Tacitus; of modern writers, Ju- nius most strongly reminds us of Rochefoucauld. Some examples from both are given in the notes to this trans- lation. It is curious to see how the expressions of the bitterest writer of English political satire to a great ex- tent express the same ideas as the great French satirist of private life. Had space permitted the parallel could have been drawn very closely, and much of the invective of Junius traced to its source in Rochefou- cauld.

One of the persons whom Rochefoucauld patronised and protected, was the great French fabulist, La Fontaine. This patronage was repaid by La Fontaine giving, in one of his fables, L'Homme et son Image,” an elaborate defence of his patron. After there depict- ing a man who fancied himself one of the most lovely in the world, and who complained he always found all mirrors untrustworthy, at last discovered his real image reflected in the water.

It is just this: the book is a mirror in which we all see ourselves. This has made it so unpopular. It is too true. We dislike to be told of our faults, while we only like to be told of our neighbour's. Notwithstanding Rousseau's assertion, it is young men, who, before they know their own faults and only know their neighbours', that read and tho- roughly appreciate Rochefoucauld.

After so many varied opinions he then pleases us more and seems far truer than he is in reality, it is impossible to give any general conclusion of such distinguished writers on the subject. Each reader will form his own opinion of the merits of the author and his book. To some, both will seem deserving of the highest praise; to others both will seem deserving of the highest censure. The truest judgment as to the author will be found in the remarks of a countryman of his own, as to the book in the remarks of a countryman of ours.

As to the book, Mr. Hallam says:--Among the books in ancient and modern times which record the conclusions of observing men on the moral qualities of their fellows, a high place should be reserved for the Maxims of Rochefoucauld.

REFLECTIONS; OR, SENTENCES AND MORAL MAXIMS

Our virtues are most frequently but vices disguised.

[This epigraph which is the key to the system of La Rochefoucauld, is found in another form as No. 179 of the maxims of the first edition, 1665, it is omitted from the 2nd and 3rd, and reappears for the first time in the 4th edition, in 1675, as at present, at the head of the Reflections.--AIM?MARTIN. Its best answer is ar- rived at by reversing the predicate and the subject, and you at once form a contradictory maxim equally true, our vices are most frequently but virtues disguised.]

1.--What we term virtue is often but a mass of various actions and divers interests, which fortune, or our own industry, manage to arrange; and it is not always from valour or from chastity that men are brave, and women chaste.

Who combats bravely is not therefore brave, He dreads a death-bed like the meanest slave; Who reasons wisely is not therefore wise, His pride in reasoning, not in acting, lies.” Pope, MORAL ESSAYS, Ep. i. line 115.

2.--Self-love is the greatest of flatterers.

3.--Whatever discoveries have been made in the region of self-love, there remain many unexplored ter- ritories there.

[This is the first hint of the system the author tries to develope. He wishes to find in vice a motive for all our actions, but this does not suffice him; he is obliged to call other passions to the help of his system and to confound pride, vanity, interest and egotism with self love. This confusion destroys the unity of his principle.--AIM?MARTIN.]

4.--Self love is more cunning than the most cunning man in the world.

5.--The duration of our passions is no more de- pendant upon us than the duration of our life. [Then what becomes of free will?--AIM?MARTIN]

6.--Passion often renders the most clever man a fool, and even sometimes renders the most foolish man clever.

7.--Great and striking actions which dazzle the eyes are represented by politicians as the effect of great designs, instead of which they are commonly caused by the temper and the passions. Thus the war between Augustus and Anthony, which is set down to the ambition they entertained of making themselves masters of the world, was probably but an effect of jealousy.

8.--The passions are the only advocates which always persuade. They are a natural art, the rules of which are infallible; and the simplest man with passion will be more persuasive than the most eloquent without.

[See Maxim 249 which is an illustration of this.]

9.--The passions possess a certain injustice and self interest which makes it dangerous to follow them, and in reality we should distrust them even when they appear most trustworthy.

10.--In the human heart there is a perpetual gene- ration of passions; so that the ruin of one is almost always the foundation of another.

11.--Passions often produce their contraries: ava- rice sometimes leads to prodigality, and prodigality to avarice; we are often obstinate through weakness and daring though timidity.

12.--Whatever care we take to conceal our pas- sions under the appearances of piety and honour, they are always to be seen through these veils.

[The 1st edition, 1665, preserves the image perhaps better-- “however we may conceal our passions under the veil, etc., there is always some place where they peep out.”]

13.--Our self love endures more impatiently the condemnation of our tastes than of our opinions.

14.--Men are not only prone to forget benefits and injuries; they even hate those who have obliged them, and cease to hate those who have injured them. The necessity of revenging an injury or of recompensing a benefit seems a slavery to which they are unwilling to submit.

15.--The clemency of Princes is often but policy to win the affections of the people.

So many are the advantages which monarchs gain by clemency, so greatly does it raise their fame and endear them to their subjects, that it is generally happy for them to have an opportunity of displaying it.”-- Montesquieu, ESPRIT DES LOIS, LIB. VI., C. 21.]

16.--This clemency of which they make a merit, arises oftentimes from vanity, sometimes from idle- ness, oftentimes from fear, and almost always from all three combined.

[La Rochefoucauld is content to paint the age in which he lived. Here the clemency spoken of is nothing more than an expression of the policy of Anne of Austria. Rochefoucauld had sacrificed all to her; even the favour of Cardinal Richelieu, but when she became regent she be- stowed her favours upon those she hated; her friends were forgotten.--AIM?MARTIN. The reader will hereby see that the age in which the writer lived best interprets his maxims.]

17.--The moderation of those who are happy arises from the calm which good fortune bestows upon their temper.

18.--Moderation is caused by the fear of exciting the envy and contempt which those merit who are intoxicated with their good fortune; it is a vain display of our strength of mind, and in short the mo- deration of men at their greatest height is only a desire to appear greater than their fortune.

19.--We have all sufficient strength to support the misfortunes of others.

[The strongest example of this is the passage in Lucre- tius, lib. ii., line I:-- “Suave mari magno turbantibus aequora ventis E terra magnum alterius spectare laborem.”]

20.--The constancy of the wise is only the talent of concealing the agitation of their hearts.

[Thus wisdom is only hypocrisy, says a commentator. This definition of constancy is a result of maxim 18.]

21.--Those who are condemned to death affect some- times a constancy and contempt for death which is only the fear of facing it; so that one may say that this constancy and contempt are to their mind what the bandage is to their eyes.

[See this thought elaborated in maxim 504.]

22.--Philosophy triumphs easily over past evils and future evils; but present evils triumph over it.

23.--Few people know death, we only endure it, usually from determination, and even from stupidity and custom; and most men only die because they know not how to prevent dying.

24.--When great men permit themselves to be cast down by the continuance of misfortune, they show us that they were only sustained by ambition, and not by their mind; so that PLUS a great vanity, heroes are made like other men.

[Both these maxims have been rewritten and made conciser by the author; the variations are not worth quoting.]

25.--We need greater virtues to sustain good than evil fortune.

["Prosperity do{th} best discover vice, but adversity do{th} best discover virtue."--Lord Bacon, ESSAYS{, (1625), "Of Adversity".}]

{The quotation wrongly had "does" for "doth".}

26.--Neither the sun nor death can be looked at without winking.

27.--People are often vain of their passions, even of the worst, but envy is a passion so timid and shame-faced that no one ever dare avow her.

28.--Jealousy is in a manner just and reasonable, as it tends to preserve a good which belongs, or which we believe belongs to us, on the other hand envy is a fury which cannot endure the happiness of others.

29.--The evil that we do does not attract to us so much persecution and hatred as our good qualities.

30.--We have more strength than will; and it is often merely for an excuse we say things are impos- sible.

31.--If we had no faults we should not take so much pleasure in noting those of others.

32.--Jealousy lives upon doubt; and comes to an end or becomes a fury as soon as it passes from doubt to certainty.

33.--Pride indemnifies itself and loses nothing even when it casts away vanity.

[See maxim 450, where the author states, what we take from our other faults we add to our pride.]

34.--If we had no pride we should not complain of that of others.

[The proud are ever most provoked by pride;-Cow- per, CONVERSATION 160.]

35.--Pride is much the same in all men, the only difference is the method and manner of showing it.

[Pride bestowed on all a common friend;--Pope, ESSAY ON MAN, Ep. ii., line 273.]

36.--It would seem that nature, which has so wisely ordered the organs of our body for our happiness, has also given us pride to spare us the mortification of knowing our imperfections.

37.--Pride has a larger part than goodness in our remonstrances with those who commit faults, and we reprove them not so much to correct as to persuade them that we ourselves are free from faults.

38.--We promise according to our hopes; we per- form according to our fears.

[The reason why the Cardinal (Mazarin) deferred so long to grant the favours he had promised, was because he was persuaded that hope was much more capable of keeping men to their duty than gratitude.”--FRAGMENTS HISTORIQUES. RACINE.]

39.--Interest speaks all sorts of tongues and plays all sorts of characters; even that of disinterestedness.

40.--Interest blinds some and makes some see.

41.--Those who apply themselves too closely to little things often become incapable of great things.

42.--We have not enough strength to follow all our reason.

43.--A man often believes himself leader when he is led; as his mind endeavours to reach one goal, his heart insensibly drags him towards another.

44.--Strength and weakness of mind are mis-named; they are really only the good or happy arrangement of our bodily organs.

45.--The caprice of our temper is even more whim- sical than that of Fortune.

46.--The attachment or indifference which philoso- phers have shown to life is only the style of their self love, about which we can no more dispute than of that of the palate or of the choice of colours.

47.--Our temper sets a price upon every gift that we receive from fortune.

48.--Happiness is in the taste, and not in the things themselves; we are happy from possessing what we like, not from possessing what others like.

49.--We are never so happy or so unhappy as we suppose.

50.--Those who think they have merit persuade themselves that they are honoured by being unhappy, in order to persuade others and themselves that they are worthy to be the butt of fortune.

[Ambition has been so strong as to make very miserable men take comfort that they were supreme in misery; and certain it is{, that where} we cannot distinguish ourselves by some- thing excellent, we begin to take a complacency in some singular infirmities, follies, or defects of one kind or other.” --Burke, {ON THE SUBLIME AND BEAUTIFUL, (1756), Part I, Sect. XVII}.]

{The translators' incorrectly cite SPEECH ON CONCILIATION WITH AMERICA. Also, Burke does not actually write “Ambition has been...”, he writes “It has been...” when speaking of ambition.}

51.--Nothing should so much diminish the satisfac- tion which we feel with ourselves as seeing that we disapprove at one time of that which we approve of at another.

52.--Whatever difference there appears in our for- tunes, there is nevertheless a certain compensation of good and evil which renders them equal.

53.--Whatever great advantages nature may give, it is not she alone, but fortune also that makes the hero.

54.--The contempt of riches in philosophers was only a hidden desire to avenge their merit upon the injustice of fortune, by despising the very goods of which fortune had deprived them; it was a secret to guard themselves against the degradation of poverty, it was a back way by which to arrive at that distinc- tion which they could not gain by riches.

[It is always easy as well as agreeable for the inferior ranks of mankind to claim merit from the contempt of that pomp and pleasure which fortune has placed beyond their reach. The virtue of the primitive Christians, like that of the first Romans, was very frequently guarded by poverty and ignorance.”--Gibbon, DECLINE AND FALL, CHAP. 15.]

55.--The hate of favourites is only a love of favour. The envy of NOT possessing it, consoles and softens its regrets by the contempt it evinces for those who pos- sess it, and we refuse them our homage, not being able to detract from them what attracts that of the rest of the world.

56.--To establish ourselves in the world we do everything to appear as if we were established.

57.--Although men flatter themselves with their great actions, they are not so often the result of a great design as of chance.

58.--It would seem that our actions have lucky or unlucky stars to which they owe a great part of the blame or praise which is given them.

59.--There are no accidents so unfortunate from which skilful men will not draw some advantage, nor so fortunate that foolish men will not turn them to their hurt.

60.--Fortune turns all things to the advantage of those on whom she smiles.

61.--The happiness or unhappiness of men depends no less upon their dispositions than their fortunes.

[Still to ourselves in every place consigned Our own felicity we make or find.” Goldsmith, TRAVELLER, 431.]

62.--Sincerity is an openness of heart; we find it in very few people; what we usually see is only an artful dissimulation to win the confidence of others.

63.--The aversion to lying is often a hidden ambi- tion to render our words credible and weighty, and to attach a religious aspect to our conversation.

64.--Truth does not do as much good in the world, as its counterfeits do evil.

65.--There is no praise we have not lavished upon Prudence; and yet she cannot assure to us the most trifling event.

[The author corrected this maxim several times, in 1665 it is No. 75; 1666, No. 66; 1671-5, No. 65; in the last edition it stands as at present. In the first he quotes Juvenal, Sat. X., line 315. “ Nullum numen habes si sit Prudentia, nos te; Nos facimus, Fortuna, deam, coeloque locamus.” Applying to Prudence what Juvenal does to Fortune, and with much greater force.]

66.--A clever man ought to so regulate his interests that each will fall in due order. Our greediness so often troubles us, making us run after so many things at the same time, that while we too eagerly look after the least we miss the greatest.

67.--What grace is to the body good sense is to the mind.

68.--It is difficult to define love; all we can say is, that in the soul it is a desire to rule, in the mind it is a sympathy, and in the body it is a hidden and deli- cate wish to possess what we love--PLUS many mysteries.

[Love is the love of one {singularly,} with desire to be singularly beloved;-- Hobbes{, LEVIATHAN, (1651), Part I,Chapter VI}.]

{Two notes about this quotation: (1) the translators' mistakenly have “singularity” for the first “singularly” and (2) Hobbes does not actually write “Love is the...”--he writes “Love of one...” under the heading “The passion of

Love.”}

69.--If there is a pure love, exempt from the mix- ture of our other passions, it is that which is concealed at the bottom of the heart and of which even our- selves are ignorant.

70.--There is no disguise which can long hide love where it exists, nor feign it where it does not.

71.--There are few people who would not be ashamed of being beloved when they love no longer.

72.--If we judge of love by the majority of its results it rather resembles hatred than friendship.

73.--We may find women who have never indulged in an intrigue, but it is rare to find those who have intrigued but once.

[“Yet there are some, they say, who have had {NONE}; But those who have, ne'er end with only {ONE}.” {--Lord Byron, }DON JUAN, {Canto} iii., stanza 4.]

74.--There is only one sort of love, but there are a thousand different copies.

75.--Neither love nor fire can subsist without per- petual motion; both cease to live so soon as they cease to hope, or to fear.

[So Lord Byron{, STANZAS, (1819), stanza 3} says of Love-- “Like chiefs of faction, His life is action.”]

76.--There is real love just as there are real ghosts; every person speaks of it, few persons have seen it.

Oh Love! no habitant of earth thou art-- An unseen seraph, we believe in thee-- A faith whose martyrs are the broken heart,-- But never yet hath seen, nor e'er shall see The naked eye, thy form as it should be.” {--Lord Byron, }CHILDE HAROLD, {Canto} iv., stanza 121.]

77.--Love lends its name to an infinite number of engagements (COMMERCES) which are attributed to it, but with which it has no more concern than the Doge has with all that is done in Venice.

78.--The love of justice is simply in the majority of men the fear of suffering injustice.

79.--Silence is the best resolve for him who distrusts himself.

80.--What renders us so changeable in our friend- ship is, that it is difficult to know the qualities of the soul, but easy to know those of the mind.

81.--We can love nothing but what agrees with us, and we can only follow our taste or our pleasure when we prefer our friends to ourselves; nevertheless it is only by that preference that friendship can be true and perfect.

82.--Reconciliation with our enemies is but a desire to better our condition, a weariness of war, the fear of some unlucky accident.

[“Thus terminated that famous war of the Fronde. * * The Duke de la Rochefoucauld desired peace because of his dangerous wounds and ruined castles, which had made him dread even worse events. On the other side the Queen, who had shown herself so ungrateful to her too ambitious friends, did not cease to feel the bitterness of their resentment. ‘I wish,’ said she, ‘it were always night, because daylight shows me so many who have betrayed me.’”--MEMOIRES DE MADAME DE MOTTEVILLE, TOM. IV., p. 60. Another proof that although these maxims are in some cases of universal application, they were based entirely on the experience of the age in which the author lived.]

83.--What men term friendship is merely a partner- ship with a collection of reciprocal interests, and an exchange of favours--in fact it is but a trade in which self love always expects to gain something.

84.--It is more disgraceful to distrust than to be deceived by our friends.

85.--We often persuade ourselves to love people who are more powerful than we are, yet interest alone produces our friendship; we do not give our hearts away for the good we wish to do, but for that we ex- pect to receive.

86.--Our distrust of another justifies his deceit.

87.--Men would not live long in society were they not the dupes of each other.

[A maxim, adds Aim?Martin, “Which may enter into the code of a vulgar rogue, but one is astonished to find it in a moral treatise.” Yet we have scriptural authority for it: “Deceiving and being deceived.”--2 TIM. iii. 13.]

88.--Self love increases or diminishes for us the good qualities of our friends, in proportion to the satisfaction we feel with them, and we judge of their merit by the manner in which they act towards us.

89.--Everyone blames his memory, no one blames his judgment.

90.--In the intercourse of life, we please more by our faults than by our good qualities.

91.--The largest ambition has the least appearance of ambition when it meets with an absolute impossi- bility in compassing its object.

92.--To awaken a man who is deceived as to his own merit is to do him as bad a turn as that done to the Athenian madman who was happy in believing that all the ships touching at the port belonged to him.

[That is, they cured him. The madman was Thrasyllus, son of Pythodorus. His brother Crito cured him, when he infinitely regretted the time of his more pleasant mad- ness.--See Aelian, VAR. HIST. iv. 25. So Horace-- ------------- “Pol, me occidistis, amici, Non servastis,” ait, “cui sic extorta voluptas Et demptus per vim mentis gratissimus error.” HOR. EP. ii--2, 138, of the madman who was cured of a pleasant lunacy.]

93.--Old men delight in giving good advice as a consolation for the fact that they can no longer set bad examples.

94.--Great names degrade instead of elevating those who know not how to sustain them.

95.--The test of extraordinary merit is to see those who envy it the most yet obliged to praise it.

96.--A man is perhaps ungrateful, but often less chargeable with ingratitude than his benefactor is.

97.--We are deceived if we think that mind and judgment are two different matters: judgment is but the extent of the light of the mind. This light penetrates to the bottom of matters; it remarks all that can be remarked, and perceives what appears imper- ceptible. Therefore we must agree that it is the ex- tent of the light in the mind that produces all the effects which we attribute to judgment.

98.--Everyone praises his heart, none dare praise their understanding.

99.--Politeness of mind consists in thinking chaste and refined thoughts.

100.--Gallantry of mind is saying the most empty things in an agreeable manner.

101.--Ideas often flash across our minds more com- plete than we could make them after much labour.

102.--The head is ever the dupe of the heart.

[A feeble imitation of that great thought “All folly comes from the heart.”--AIM?MARTIN. But Bonhome, in his L'ART DE PENSER, says “Plusieurs diraient en periode quarr que quelques reflexions que fasse l'esprit et quelques resolu- tions qu'il prenne pour corriger ses travers le premier sen- timent du coeur renverse tous ses projets. Mais il n'appar- tient qu'a M. de la Rochefoucauld de dire tout en un mot que l'esprit est toujours la dupe du coeur.”]

103.--Those who know their minds do not neces- sarily know their hearts.

104.--Men and things have each their proper per- spective; to judge rightly of some it is necessary to see them near, of others we can never judge rightly but at a distance.

105.--A man for whom accident discovers sense, is not a rational being. A man only is so who under- stands, who distinguishes, who tests it.

106.--To understand matters rightly we should understand their details, and as that knowledge is almost infinite, our knowledge is always superficial and imperfect.

107.--One kind of flirtation is to boast we never flirt.

108.--The head cannot long play the part of the heart.

109.--Youth changes its tastes by the warmth of its blood, age retains its tastes by habit.

110.--Nothing is given so profusely as advice.

111.--The more we love a woman the more prone we are to hate her.

112.--The blemishes of the mind, like those of the face, increase by age.

113.--There may be good but there are no pleasant marriages.

114.--We are inconsolable at being deceived by our enemies and betrayed by our friends, yet still we are often content to be thus served by ourselves.

115.--It is as easy unwittingly to deceive oneself as to deceive others.

116.--Nothing is less sincere than the way of asking and giving advice. The person asking seems to pay deference to the opinion of his friend, while thinking in reality of making his friend approve his opinion and be responsible for his conduct. The person giving the advice returns the confidence placed in him by eager and disinterested zeal, in doing which he is usually guided only by his own interest or reputation.

[I have often thought how ill-natured a maxim it was which on many occasions I have heard from people of good understanding, ‘That as to what related to private conduct no one was ever the better for advice.’ But upon further examination I have resolved with myself that the maxim might be admitted without any violent prejudice to mankind. For in the manner advice was generally given there was no reason I thought to wonder it should be so ill received, something there was which strangely inverted the case, and made the giver to be the only gainer. For by what I could observe in many occurrences of our lives, that which we called giving advice was properly taking an occasion to show our own wisdom at another's expense. On the other side to be instructed or to receive advice on the terms usually prescribed to us was little better than tamely to afford another the occasion of raising himself a character from our defects;--Lord Shaftesbury, CHARAC- TERISTICS, i., 153.]

117.--The most subtle of our acts is to simulate blindness for snares that we know are set for us. We are never so easily deceived as when trying to deceive.

118.--The intention of never deceiving often exposes us to deception.

119.--We become so accustomed to disguise ourselves to others that at last we are disguised to ourselves.

[Those who quit their proper character{,} to assume what does not belong to them, are{,} for the greater part{,} ignorant both of the character they leave{,} and of the character they assume.”--Burke, {REFLECTIONS ON THE REVOLUTION IN FRANCE, (1790), Paragraph 19}.]

{The translators' incorrectly cite THOUGHTS ON THE CAUSE OF THE PRESENT DISCONTENTS.}

120.--We often act treacherously more from weak- ness than from a fixed motive.

121.--We frequently do good to enable us with impunity to do evil.

122.--If we conquer our passions it is more from their weakness than from our strength.

123.--If we never flattered ourselves we should have but scant pleasure.

124.--The most deceitful persons spend their lives in blaming deceit, so as to use it on some great occa- sion to promote some great interest.

125.--The daily employment of cunning marks a little mind, it generally happens that those who resort to it in one respect to protect themselves lay them- selves open to attack in another.

[With that low cunning which in fools supplies, And amply, too, the place of being wise; Churchill, ROSCIAD, 117.]

126.--Cunning and treachery are the offspring of incapacity.

127.--The true way to be deceived is to think one- self more knowing than others.

128.--Too great cleverness is but deceptive delicacy, true delicacy is the most substantial cleverness.

129.--It is sometimes necessary to play the fool to avoid being deceived by cunning men.

130.--Weakness is the only fault which cannot be cured.

131.--The smallest fault of women who give them- selves up to love is to love. [------Faciunt graviora coactae Imperio sexus minimumque libidine peccant; Juvenal, SAT. vi., 134.]

132.--It is far easier to be wise for others than to be so for oneself.

[Hence the proverb,;A man who is his own lawyer has a fool for his client;]

133.--The only good examples are those, that make us see the absurdity of bad originals.

134.--We are never so ridiculous from the habits we have as from those that we affect to have.

135.--We sometimes differ more widely from our- selves than we do from others.

136.--There are some who never would have loved if they never had heard it spoken of.

137.--When not prompted by vanity we say little.

138.--A man would rather say evil of himself than say nothing.

[Montaigne's vanity led him to talk perpetually of himself, and as often happens to vain men, he would rather talk of his own failings than of any foreign subject.”-- Hallam, LITERATURE OF EUROPE.]

139.--One of the reasons that we find so few persons rational and agreeable in conversation is there is hardly a person who does not think more of what he wants to say than of his answer to what is said. The most clever and polite are content with only seeming attentive while we perceive in their mind and eyes that at the very time they are wander- ing from what is said and desire to return to what they want to say. Instead of considering that the worst way to persuade or please others is to try thus strongly to please ourselves, and that to listen well and to answer well are some of the greatest charms we can have in conversation.

[“An absent man can make but few observations, he can pursue nothing steadily because his absences make him lose his way. They are very disagreeable and hardly to be tolerated in old age, but in youth they cannot be forgiven.” --Lord Chesterfield, LETTER 195.]

140.--If it was not for the company of fools, a witty man would often be greatly at a loss.

141.--We often boast that we are never bored, but yet we are so conceited that we do not perceive how often we bore others.

142.--As it is the mark of great minds to say many things in a few words, so it is that of little minds to use many words to say nothing.

["So much they talked, so very little said." Churchill, ROSCIAD, 550.

"Men who are unequal to the labour of discussing an ar- gument or wish to avoid it, are willing enough to suppose that much has been proved because much has been said."-- Junius, JAN. 1769.]

143.--It is oftener by the estimation of our own feelings that we exaggerate the good qualities of others than by their merit, and when we praise them we wish to attract their praise.

144.--We do not like to praise, and we never praise without a motive. Praise is flattery, artful, hidden, delicate, which gratifies differently him who praises and him who is praised. The one takes it as the re- ward of merit, the other bestows it to show his im- partiality and knowledge.

145.--We often select envenomed praise which, by a reaction upon those we praise, shows faults we could not have shown by other means.

146.--Usually we only praise to be praised.

147.--Few are sufficiently wise to prefer censure which is useful to praise which is treacherous.

148.--Some reproaches praise; some praises re- proach.

["Damn with faint praise, assent with civil leer, And, without sneering, teach the rest to sneer." Pope {ESSAY ON MAN, (1733), EPISTLE TO DR. ARBUTHNOT.}]

149.--The refusal of praise is only the wish to be praised twice.

[The modesty which pretends to refuse praise is but in truth a desire to be praised more highly. EDITION 1665.]

150.--The desire which urges us to deserve praise strengthens our good qualities, and praise given to wit, valour, and beauty, tends to increase them.

151.--It is easier to govern others than to prevent being governed.

152.--If we never flattered ourselves the flattery of others would not hurt us.

[“Adulatione servilia fingebant securi de fragilitate cre-dentis.” Tacit. Ann. xvi.]

153.--Nature makes merit but fortune sets it to work.

154.--Fortune cures us of many faults that reason could not.

155.--There are some persons who only disgust with their abilities, there are persons who please even with their faults.

156.--There are persons whose only merit consists in saying and doing stupid things at the right time, and who ruin all if they change their manners.

157.--The fame of great men ought always to be estimated by the means used to acquire it.

158.--Flattery is base coin to which only our vanity gives currency.

159.--It is not enough to have great qualities, we should also have the management of them.

160.--However brilliant an action it should not be esteemed great unless the result of a great motive.

161.--A certain harmony should be kept between actions and ideas if we desire to estimate the effects that they produce.

162.--The art of using moderate abilities to advan- tage wins praise, and often acquires more reputation than real brilliancy.

163.--Numberless arts appear foolish whose secre{t} motives are most wise and weighty.

164.--It is much easier to seem fitted for posts we do not fill than for those we do.

165.--Ability wins us the esteem of the true men, luck that of the people.

166.--The world oftener rewards the appearance of merit than merit itself.

167.--Avarice is more opposed to economy than to liberality.

168.--However deceitful hope may be, yet she carries us on pleasantly to the end of life.

[“Hope travels through, nor quits us when we die.” Pope: ESSAY ON MAN, Ep. ii.]

169.--Idleness and fear keeps us in the path of duty, but our virtue often gets the praise.

[“Quod segnitia erat sapientia vocaretur.” Tacitus Hist. I.]

170.--If one acts rightly and honestly, it is difficult to decide whether it is the effect of integrity or skill.

171.--As rivers are lost in the sea so are virtues in self.

172.--If we thoroughly consider the varied effects of indifference we find we miscarry more in our duties than in our interests.

173.--There are different kinds of curiosity: one springs from interest, which makes us desire to know everything that may be profitable to us; another from pride, which springs from a desire of knowing what others are ignorant of.

174.--It is far better to accustom our mind to bear the ills we have than to speculate on those which may befall us.

[“Rather bear th{ose} ills we have Than fly to others that we know not of.” {--Shakespeare, HAMLET, Act III, Scene I, Hamlet.}]

175.--Constancy in love is a perpetual inconstancy which causes our heart to attach itself to all the quali- ties of the person we love in succession, sometimes giving the preference to one, sometimes to another. This constancy is merely inconstancy fixed, and limited to the same person.

176.--There are two kinds of constancy in love, one arising from incessantly finding in the loved one fresh objects to love, the other from regarding it as a point of honour to be constant.

177.--Perseverance is not deserving of blame or praise, as it is merely the continuance of tastes and feelings which we can neither create or destroy.

178.--What makes us like new studies is not so much the weariness we have of the old or the wish for change as the desire to be admired by those who know more than ourselves, and the hope of advantage over those who know less.

179.--We sometimes complain of the levity of our friends to justify our own by anticipation.

180.--Our repentance is not so much sorrow for the ill we have done as fear of the ill that may happen to us.

181.--One sort of inconstancy springs from levity or weakness of mind, and makes us accept everyone's opinion, and another more excusable comes from a surfeit of matter.

182.--Vices enter into the composition of virtues as poison into that of medicines. Prudence collects and blends the two and renders them useful against the ills of life.

183.--For the credit of virtue we must admit that the greatest misfortunes of men are those into which they fall through their crimes.

184.--We admit our faults to repair by our sincerity the evil we have done in the opinion of others.

[In the edition of 1665 this maxim stands as No. 200. We never admit our faults except through vanity.]

185.--There are both heroes of evil and heroes of good.

[Ut alios industria ita hunc ignavia protulerat ad famam, habebaturque non ganeo et profligator sed erudito luxu. --Tacit. Ann. xvi.]

186.--We do not despise all who have vices, but we do despise all who have not virtues.

[“If individuals have no virtues their vices may be of use to us.”--JUNIUS, 5th Oct. 1771.]

187.--The name of virtue is as useful to our interest as that of vice.

188.--The health of the mind is not less uncertain than that of the body, and when passions seem furthest removed we are no less in danger of infec- tion than of falling ill when we are well.

189.--It seems that nature has at man's birth fixed the bounds of his virtues and vices.

190.--Great men should not have great faults.

191.--We may say vices wait on us in the course of our life as the landlords with whom we successively lodge, and if we travelled the road twice over I doubt if our experience would make us avoid them.

192.--When our vices leave us we flatter ourselves with the idea we have left them.

193.--There are relapses in the diseases of the mind as in those of the body; what we call a cure is often no more than an intermission or change of disease.

194.--The defects of the mind are like the wounds of the body. Whatever care we take to heal them the scars ever remain, and there is always danger of their reopening.

195.--The reason which often prevents us abandon- ing a single vice is having so many.

196.--We easily forget those faults which are known only to ourselves.

[Seneca says “Innocentem quisque se dicit respiciens testem non conscientiam.”]

197.--There are men of whom we can never believe evil without having seen it. Yet there are very few in whom we should be surprised to see it.

198.--We exaggerate the glory of some men to detract from that of others, and we should praise Prince Cond?and Marshal Turenne much less if we did not want to blame them both.

[The allusion to Cond?and Turenne gives the date at which these maxims were published in 1665. Cond?and Turenne were after their campaign with the Imperialists at the height of their fame. It proves the truth of the remark of Tacitus, “Populus neminem sine aemulo sinit.”-- Tac. Ann. xiv.]

199.--The desire to appear clever often prevents our being so.

200.--Virtue would not go far did not vanity escort her.

201.--He who thinks he has the power to content the world greatly deceives himself, but he who thinks that the world cannot be content with him deceives himself yet more.

202.--Falsely honest men are those who disguise their faults both to themselves and others; truly honest men are those who know them perfectly and confess them.

203.--He is really wise who is nettled at nothing.

204.--The coldness of women is a balance and bur- den they add to their beauty.

205.--Virtue in woman is often the love of reputa- tion and repose.

206.--He is a truly good man who desires always to bear the inspection of good men.

207.--Folly follows us at all stages of life. If one appears wise 'tis but because his folly is proportioned to his age and fortune.

208.--There are foolish people who know and who skilfully use their folly.

209.--Who lives without folly is not so wise as he thinks.

210.--In growing old we become more foolish--and more wise.

211.--There are people who are like farces, which are praised but for a time (however foolish and dis- tasteful they may be).

[The last clause is added from Edition of 1665.]

212.--Most people judge men only by success or by fortune.

213.--Love of glory, fear of shame, greed of fortune, the desire to make life agreeable and comfortable, and the wish to depreciate others are often causes of that bravery so vaunted among men.

[Junius said of the Marquis of Granby, "He was as brave as a total absence of all feeling and reflection could make him."--21st Jan. 1769.]

214.--Valour in common soldiers is a perilous method of earning their living.

["Men venture necks to gain a fortune, The soldier does it ev{'}ry day, (Eight to the week) for sixpence pay." {--Samuel Butler,} HUDIBRAS, Part II., canto i., line 512.]

215.--Perfect bravery and sheer cowardice are two extremes rarely found. The space between them is vast, and embraces all other sorts of courage. The difference between them is not less than between faces and tempers. Men will freely expose themselves at the beginning of an action, and relax and be easily discouraged if it should last. Some are content to satisfy worldly honour, and beyond that will do little else. Some are not always equally masters of their timidity. Others allow themselves to be overcome by panic; others charge because they dare not remain at their posts. Some may be found whose courage is strengthened by small perils, which prepare them to face greater dangers. Some will dare a sword cut and flinch from a bullet; others dread bullets little and fear to fight with swords. These varied kinds of courage agree in this, that night, by increasing fear and conceal- ing gallant or cowardly actions, allows men to spare themselves. There is even a more general discretion to be observed, for we meet with no man who does all he would have done if he were assured of getting off scot-free; so that it is certain that the fear of death does somewhat subtract from valour.

[See also “Table Talk of Napoleon,” who agrees with this, so far as to say that few, but himself, had a two o'clock of the morning valour.]

216.--Perfect valour is to do without witnesses what one would do before all the world.

[“It is said of untrue valours that some men's valours are in the eyes of them that look on.”--Bacon, ADVANCEMENT OF LEARNING{, (1605), Book I, Section II, paragraph 5}.]

217.--Intrepidity is an extraordinary strength of soul which raises it above the troubles, disorders, and emotions which the sight of great perils can arouse in it: by this strength heroes maintain a calm aspect and preserve their reason and liberty in the most sur- prising and terrible accidents.

218.--Hypocrisy is the homage vice pays to virtue.

[So Massillon, in one of his sermons, “Vice pays homage to virtue in doing honour to her appearance.”

So Junius, writing to the Duke of Grafton, says, "You have done as much mischief to the community as Machia- vel, if Machiavel had not known that an appearance of morals and religion are useful in society."--28 Sept. 1771.]

219.--Most men expose themselves in battle enough to save their honor, few wish to do so more than sufficiently, or than is necessary to make the design for which they expose themselves succeed.

220.--Vanity, shame, and above all disposition, often make men brave and women chaste.

["Vanity bids all her sons be brave and all her daughters chaste and courteous. But why do we need her instruc- tion?"--Sterne, SERMONS.]

221.--We do not wish to lose life; we do wish to gain glory, and this makes brave men show more tact and address in avoiding death, than rogues show in preserving their fortunes.

222.--Few persons on the first approach of age do not show wherein their body, or their mind, is begin- ning to fail.

223.--Gratitude is as the good faith of merchants: it holds commerce together; and we do not pay be- cause it is just to pay debts, but because we shall thereby more easily find people who will lend.

224.--All those who pay the debts of gratitude can- not thereby flatter themselves that they are grateful.

225.--What makes false reckoning, as regards gra- titude, is that the pride of the giver and the receiver cannot agree as to the value of the benefit.

["The first foundation of friendship is not the power of conferring benefits, but the equality with which they are received, and may be returned."--Junius's LETTER TO THE KING.]

226.--Too great a hurry to discharge of an obliga- tion is a kind of ingratitude.

227.--Lucky people are bad hands at correcting their faults; they always believe that they are right when fortune backs up their vice or folly.

[“The power of fortune is confessed only by the misera- ble, for the happy impute all their success to prudence and merit.”--Swift, THOUGHTS ON VARIOUS SUBJECTS]

228.--Pride will not owe, self-love will not pay.

229.--The good we have received from a man should make us excuse the wrong he does us.

230.--Nothing is so infectious as example, and we never do great good or evil without producing the like. We imitate good actions by emulation, and bad ones by the evil of our nature, which shame imprisons until example liberates.

231.--It is great folly to wish only to be wise.

232.--Whatever pretext we give to our afflictions it is always interest or vanity that causes them.

233.--In afflictions there are various kinds of hypo- crisy. In one, under the pretext of weeping for one dear to us we bemoan ourselves; we regret her good opinion of us, we deplore the loss of our comfort, our pleasure, our consideration. Thus the dead have the credit of tears shed for the living. I affirm 'tis a kind of hypocrisy which in these afflictions deceives itself. There is another kind not so innocent because it im- poses on all the world, that is the grief of those who aspire to the glory of a noble and immortal sorrow. After Time, which absorbs all, has obliterated what sorrow they had, they still obstinately obtrude their tears, their sighs their groans, they wear a solemn face, and try to persuade others by all their acts, that their grief will end only with their life. This sad and distressing vanity is commonly found in ambitious women. As their sex closes to them all paths to glory, they strive to render themselves celebrated by show- ing an inconsolable affliction. There is yet another kind of tears arising from but small sources, which flow easily and cease as easily. One weeps to achieve a reputation for tenderness, weeps to be pitied, weeps to be bewept, in fact one weeps to avoid the disgrace of not weeping!

[“In grief the {PLEASURE} is still uppermost{;} and the afflic- tion we suffer has no resemblance to absolute pain which is always odious, and which we endeavour to shake off as soon as possible.”--Burke, SUBLIME AND BEAUTIFUL{, (1756), Part I, Sect. V}.]

234.--It is more often from pride than from igno- rance that we are so obstinately opposed to current opinions; we find the first places taken, and we do not want to be the last.

235.--We are easily consoled at the misfortunes of our friends when they enable us to prove our tender- ness for them.

236.--It would seem that even self-love may be the dupe of goodness and forget itself when we work for others. And yet it is but taking the shortest way to arrive at its aim, taking usury under the pretext of giving, in fact winning everybody in a subtle and de- licate manner.

237.--No one should be praised for his goodness if he has not strength enough to be wicked. All other goodness is but too often an idleness or powerlessness of will.

238.--It is not so dangerous to do wrong to most men, as to do them too much good.

239.--Nothing flatters our pride so much as the confidence of the great, because we regard it as the result of our worth, without remembering that gene- rally 'tis but vanity, or the inability to keep a secret.

240.--We may say of conformity as distinguished from beauty, that it is a symmetry which knows no rules, and a secret harmony of features both one with each other and with the colour and appearance of the person.

241.--Flirtation is at the bottom of woman's nature, although all do not practise it, some being restrained by fear, others by sense.

[“By nature woman is a flirt, but her flirting changes both in the mode and object according to her opinions.”-- Rousseau, EMILE.]

242.--We often bore others when we think we cannot possibly bore them.

243.--Few things are impossible in themselves; application to make them succeed fails us more often than the means.

244.--Sovereign ability consists in knowing the value of things.

245.--There is great ability in knowing how to con- ceal one's ability.

[“You have accomplished a great stroke in diplomacy when you have made others think that you have only very average abilities.”--LA BRUY 萊 E.]

246.--What seems generosity is often disguised am- bition, that despises small to run after greater inte- rest.

247.--The fidelity of most men is merely an inven- tion of self-love to win confidence; a method to place us above others and to render us depositaries of the most important matters.

248.--Magnanimity despises all, to win all.

249.--There is no less eloquence in the voice, in the eyes and in the air of a speaker than in his choice of words.

250.--True eloquence consists in saying all that should be, not all that could be said.

251.--There are people whose faults become them, others whose very virtues disgrace them.

[“There are faults which do him honour, and virtues that disgrace him.”--Junius, LETTER OF 28TH MAY, 1770.]

252.--It is as common to change one's tastes, as it is uncommon to change one's inclinations.

253.--Interest sets at work all sorts of virtues and vices.

254.--Humility is often a feigned submission which we employ to supplant others. It is one of the de- vices of Pride to lower us to raise us; and truly pride transforms itself in a thousand ways, and is never so well disguised and more able to deceive than when it hides itself under the form of humility.

[“Grave and plausible enough to be thought fit for busi- ness.”--Junius, LETTER TO THE DUKE OF GRAFTON.

“He saw a cottage with a double coach-house, A cottage of gentility, And the devil was pleased, for his darling sin Is the pride that apes humility.” Southey, DEVIL'S WALK.]

{There are numerous corrections necessary for this quotation; I will keep the original above so you can compare the correct passages:

“He passed a cottage with a double coach-house, A cottage of gentility, And he owned with a grin, That his favourite sin Is pride that apes humility.” --Southey, DEVIL'S WALK, Stanza 8.

“And the devil did grin, for his darling sin Is pride that apes humility.” --Samuel Taylor Coleridge, THE DEVIL'S THOUGHTS}

255.--All feelings have their peculiar tone of voice, gestures and looks, and this harmony, as it is good or bad, pleasant or unpleasant, makes people agreeable or disagreeable.

256.--In all professions we affect a part and an ap- pearance to seem what we wish to be. Thus the world is merely composed of actors.

[“All the world's a stage, and all the men and women merely players.”--Shakespeare, AS YOU LIKE IT{, Act II, Scene VII, Jaques}.

“Life is no more than a dramatic scene, in which the hero should preserve his consistency to the last.”--Junius.]

257.--Gravity is a mysterious carriage of the body invented to conceal the want of mind.

["Gravity is the very essence of imposture."--Shaftes- bury, CHARACTERISTICS, p. 11, vol. I. "The very essence of gravity is design, and consequently deceit; a taught trick to gain credit with the world for more sense and know- ledge than a man was worth, and that with all its preten- sions it was no better, but often worse, than what a French wit had long ago defined it--a mysterious carriage of the body to cover the defects of the mind."--Sterne, TRISTRAM SHANDY, vol. I., chap. ii.]

258.--Good taste arises more from judgment than wit.

259.--The pleasure of love is in loving, we are hap- pier in the passion we feel than in that we inspire.

260.--Civility is but a desire to receive civility, and to be esteemed polite.

261.--The usual education of young people is to in- spire them with a second self-love.

262.--There is no passion wherein self-love reigns so powerfully as in love, and one is always more ready to sacrifice the peace of the loved one than his own.

263.--What we call liberality is often but the vanity of giving, which we like more than that we give away.

264.--Pity is often a reflection of our own evils in the ills of others. It is a delicate foresight of the troubles into which we may fall. We help others that on like occasions we may be helped ourselves, and these services which we render, are in reality benefits we confer on ourselves by anticipation.

["GRIEF for the calamity of another is pity, and ariseth from the imagination that a like calamity may befal him- self{;} and therefore is called compassion."--HOBBES' LEVIA- THAN{, (1651), Part I, Chapter VI}.]

265.--A narrow mind begets obstinacy, and we do not easily believe what we cannot see.

[“Stiff in opinion, always in the wrong.” Dryden, ABSALOM AND ACHITOPHEL{, line 547}.]

266.--We deceive ourselves if we believe that there are violent passions like ambition and love that can triumph over others. Idleness, languishing as she is, does not often fail in being mistress; she usurps authority over all the plans and actions of life; im- perceptibly consuming and destroying both passions and virtues.

267.--A quickness in believing evil without having sufficiently examined it, is the effect of pride and laziness. We wish to find the guilty, and we do not wish to trouble ourselves in examining the crime.

268.--We credit judges with the meanest motives, and yet we desire our reputation and fame should depend upon the judgment of men, who are all, either from their jealousy or pre-occupation or want of in- telligence, opposed to us--and yet 'tis only to make these men decide in our favour that we peril in so many ways both our peace and our life.

269.--No man is clever enough to know all the evil he does.

270.--One honour won is a surety for more.

271.--Youth is a continual intoxication; it is the fever of reason.

[“The best of life is but intoxication.”--{Lord Byron, } Don Juan{, Canto II, stanza 179}. In the 1st Edition, 1665, the maxim finishes with-- “it is the fever of health, the folly of reason.”]

272.--Nothing should so humiliate men who have deserved great praise, as the care they have taken to acquire it by the smallest means.

273.--There are persons of whom the world approves who have no merit beyond the vices they use in the affairs of life.

274.--The beauty of novelty is to love as the flower to the fruit; it lends a lustre which is easily lost, but which never returns.

275.--Natural goodness, which boasts of being so apparent, is often smothered by the least interest.

276.--Absence extinguishes small passions and in- creases great ones, as the wind will blow out a candle, and blow in a fire.

277.--Women often think they love when they do not love. The business of a love affair, the emotion of mind that sentiment induces, the natural bias towards the pleasure of being loved, the difficulty of refusing, persuades them that they have real passion when they have but flirtation.

[“And if in fact she takes a {“}GRANDE PASSION{”}, It is a very serious thing indeed: Nine times in ten 'tis but caprice or fashion, Coquetry, or a wish to take the lead, The pride of a mere child with a new sash on. Or wish to make a rival's bosom bleed: But the {TENTH} instance will be a tornado, For there's no saying what they will or may do.” {--Lord Byron, }DON JUAN, canto xii. stanza 77.]

278.--What makes us so often discontented with those who transact business for us is that they almost always abandon the interest of their friends for the interest of the business, because they wish to have the honour of succeeding in that which they have undertaken.

279.--When we exaggerate the tenderness of our friends towards us, it is often less from gratitude than from a desire to exhibit our own merit.

280.--The praise we give to new comers into the world arises from the envy we bear to those who are established.

281.--Pride, which inspires, often serves to mode- rate envy.

282.--Some disguised lies so resemble truth, that we should judge badly were we not deceived.

283.--Sometimes there is not less ability in knowing how to use than in giving good advice.

284.--There are wicked people who would be much less dangerous if they were wholly without goodness.

285.--Magnanimity is sufficiently defined by its name, nevertheless one can say it is the good sense of pride, the most noble way of receiving praise.

286.--It is impossible to love a second time those whom we have really ceased to love.

287.--Fertility of mind does not furnish us with so many resources on the same matter, as the lack of intelligence makes us hesitate at each thing our ima- gination presents, and hinders us from at first discern- ing which is the best.

288.--There are matters and maladies which at certain times remedies only serve to make worse; true skill consists in knowing when it is dangerous to use them.

289.--Affected simplicity is refined imposture.

[Domitianus simplicitatis ac modestiae imagine studium litterarum et amorem carminum simulabat quo velaret animum et fratris aemulationi subduceretur.--Tacitus, ANN. iv.]

290.--There are as many errors of temper as of mind.

291.--Man's merit, like the crops, has its season.

292.--One may say of temper as of many buildings; it has divers aspects, some agreeable, others dis- agreeable.

293.--Moderation cannot claim the merit of op- posing and overcoming Ambition: they are never found together. Moderation is the languor and sloth of the soul, Ambition its activity and heat.

294.--We always like those who admire us, we do not always like those whom we admire.

295.--It is well that we know not all our wishes.

296.--It is difficult to love those we do not esteem, but it is no less so to love those whom we esteem much more than ourselves.

297.--Bodily temperaments have a common course and rule which imperceptibly affect our will. They advance in combination, and successively exercise a secret empire over us, so that, without our perceiving it, they become a great part of all our actions.

298.--The gratitude of most men is but a secret desire of receiving greater benefits.

[Hence the common proverb “Gratitude is merely a lively sense of favors to come.”]

299.--Almost all the world takes pleasure in paying small debts; many people show gratitude for trifling, but there is hardly one who does not show ingrati- tude for great favours.

300.--There are follies as catching as infections.

301.--Many people despise, but few know how to bestow wealth.

302.--Only in things of small value we usually are bold enough not to trust to appearances.

303.--Whatever good quality may be imputed to us, we ourselves find nothing new in it.

304.--We may forgive those who bore us, we cannot forgive those whom we bore.

305.--Interest which is accused of all our misdeeds often should be praised for our good deeds.

306.--We find very few ungrateful people when we are able to confer favours.

307.--It is as proper to be boastful alone as it is ridiculous to be so in company.

308.--Moderation is made a virtue to limit the am- bition of the great; to console ordinary people for their small fortune and equally small ability.

309.--There are persons fated to be fools, who com- mit follies not only by choice, but who are forced by fortune to do so.

310.--Sometimes there are accidents in our life the skilful extrication from which demands a little folly.

311.--If there be men whose folly has never ap- peared, it is because it has never been closely looked for.

312.--Lovers are never tired of each other,--they always speak of themselves.

313.--How is it that our memory is good enough to retain the least triviality that happens to us, and yet not good enough to recollect how often we have told it to the same person?

[“Old men who yet retain the memory of things past, and forget how often they have told them, are most tedious companions.”-- Montaigne, {ESSAYS, Book I,Chapter IX}.]

314.--The extreme delight we take in talking of ourselves should warn us that it is not shared by those who listen.

315.--What commonly hinders us from showing the recesses of our heart to our friends, is not the dis- trust we have of them, but that we have of our- selves.

316.--Weak persons cannot be sincere.

317.--'Tis a small misfortune to oblige an ungrate- ful man; but it is unbearable to be obliged by a scoundrel.

318.--We may find means to cure a fool of his folly, but there are none to set straight a cross-grained spirit.

319.--If we take the liberty to dwell on their faults we cannot long preserve the feelings we should hold towards our friends and benefactors.

320.--To praise princes for virtues they do not pos- sess is but to reproach them with impunity.

[“Praise undeserved is satire in disguise,” quoted by Pope from a poem which has not survived, “The Garland,” by Mr. Broadhurst. “In some cases exaggerated or inappropriate praise becomes the most severe satire.”-- Scott, WOODSTOCK.]

321.--We are nearer loving those who hate us, than those who love us more than we desire.

322.--Those only are despicable who fear to be despised.

323.--Our wisdom is no less at the mercy of Fortune than our goods.

324.--There is more self-love than love in jealousy.

325.--We often comfort ourselves by the weakness of evils, for which reason has not the strength to con- sole us.

326.--Ridicule dishonours more than dishonour itself.

[“No,” says a commentator, “Ridicule may do harm, but it cannot dishonour; it is vice which confers dis- honour.”]

327.--We own to small faults to persuade others that we have not great ones.

328.--Envy is more irreconcilable than hatred.

329.--We believe, sometimes, that we hate flattery --we only dislike the method.

[“{But} when I tell him he hates flatter{ers}, He says he does, being then most flattered.” Shakespeare, JULIUS CAESAR{, Act II, Scene I, Decius}.]

330.--We pardon in the degree that we love.

331.--It is more difficult to be faithful to a mistress when one is happy, than when we are ill-treated by her.

[Si qua volet regnare diu contemnat amantem.--Ovid, AMORES, ii. 19.]

332.--Women do not know all their powers of flirtation.

333.--Women cannot be completely severe unless they hate.

334.--Women can less easily resign flirtations than love.

335.--In love deceit almost always goes further than mistrust.

336.--There is a kind of love, the excess of which forbids jealousy.

337.--There are certain good qualities as there are senses, and those who want them can neither per- ceive nor understand them.

338.--When our hatred is too bitter it places us below those whom we hate.

339.--We only appreciate our good or evil in pro- portion to our self-love.

340.--The wit of most women rather strengthens their folly than their reason.

[“Women have an entertaining tattle, and sometimes wit, but for solid reasoning and good sense I never knew one in my life that had it, and who reasoned and acted conse- quentially for four and twenty hours together.”--Lord Chesterfield, LETTER 129.]

341.--The heat of youth is not more opposed to safety than the coldness of age.

342.--The accent of our native country dwells in the heart and mind as well as on the tongue.

343.--To be a great man one should know how to profit by every phase of fortune.

344.--Most men, like plants, possess hidden quali- ties which chance discovers.

345.--Opportunity makes us known to others, but more to ourselves.

346.--If a woman's temper is beyond control there can be no control of the mind or heart.

347.--We hardly find any persons of good sense, save those who agree with us.

[“That was excellently observed, say I, when I read an author when his opinion agrees with mine.”--Swift, THOUGHTS ON VARIOUS SUBJECTS.]

348.--When one loves one doubts even what one most believes.

349.--The greatest miracle of love is to eradicate flirtation.

350.--Why we hate with so much bitterness those who deceive us is because they think themselves more clever than we are.

[“I could pardon all his (Louis XI.'s) deceit, but I can- not forgive his supposing me capable of the gross folly of being duped by his professions.”--Sir Walter Scott, QUENTIN DURWARD.]

351.--We have much trouble to break with one, when we no longer are in love.

352.--We almost always are bored with persons with whom we should not be bored.

353.--A gentleman may love like a lunatic, but not like a beast.

354.--There are certain defects which well mounted glitter like virtue itself.

355.--Sometimes we lose friends for whose loss our regret is greater than our grief, and others for whom our grief is greater than our regret.

356.--Usually we only praise heartily those who admire us.

357.--Little minds are too much wounded by little things; great minds see all and are not even hurt.

358.--Humility is the true proof of Christian virtues; without it we retain all our faults, and they are only covered by pride to hide them from others, and often from ourselves.

359.--Infidelities should extinguish love, and we ought not to be jealous when we have cause to be so. No persons escape causing jealousy who are worthy of exciting it.

360.--We are more humiliated by the least infidelity towards us, than by our greatest towards others.

361.--Jealousy is always born with love, but does not always die with it.

362.--Most women do not grieve so much for the death of their lovers for love's-sake, as to show they were worthy of being beloved.

363.--The evils we do to others give us less pain than those we do to ourselves.

364.--We well know that it is bad taste to talk of our wives; but we do not so well know that it is the same to speak of ourselves.

365.--There are virtues which degenerate into vices when they arise from Nature, and others which when acquired are never perfect. For example, reason must teach us to manage our estate and our con- fidence, while Nature should have given us goodness and valour.

366.--However we distrust the sincerity of those whom we talk with, we always believe them more sin- cere with us than with others.

367.--There are few virtuous women who are not tired of their part.

["Every woman is at heart a rake."--Pope. MORAL ESSAYS, ii.]

368.--The greater number of good women are like concealed treasures, safe as no one has searched for them.

369.--The violences we put upon ourselves to escape love are often more cruel than the cruelty of those we love.

370.--There are not many cowards who know the whole of their fear.

371.--It is generally the fault of the loved one not to perceive when love ceases.

372.--Most young people think they are natural when they are only boorish and rude.

373.--Some tears after having deceived others de- ceive ourselves.

374.--If we think we love a woman for love of herself we are greatly deceived.

375.--Ordinary men commonly condemn what is beyond them.

376.--Envy is destroyed by true friendship, flirta- tion by true love.

377.--The greatest mistake of penetration is not to have fallen short, but to have gone too far.

378.--We may bestow advice, but we cannot inspire the conduct.

379.--As our merit declines so also does our taste.

380.--Fortune makes visible our virtues or our vices, as light does objects.

381.--The struggle we undergo to remain faithful to one we love is little better than infidelity.

382.--Our actions are like the rhymed ends of blank verses (BOUTS-RIM) where to each one puts what construction he pleases.

[The BOUTS-RIM was a literary game popular in the 17th and 18th centuries--the rhymed words at the end of a line being given for others to fill up. Thus Horace Walpole being given, “brook, why, crook, I,” returned the bur- lesque verse-- “I sits with my toes in a BROOK, And if any one axes me WHY? I gies 'em a rap with my CROOK, 'Tis constancy makes me, ses I.”]

383.--The desire of talking about ourselves, and of putting our faults in the light we wish them to be seen, forms a great part of our sincerity.

384.--We should only be astonished at still being able to be astonished.

385.--It is equally as difficult to be contented when one has too much or too little love.

386.--No people are more often wrong than those who will not allow themselves to be wrong.

387.--A fool has not stuff in him to be good.

388.--If vanity does not overthrow all virtues, at least she makes them totter.

389.--What makes the vanity of others unsupport- able is that it wounds our own.

390.--We give up more easily our interest than our taste.

391.--Fortune appears so blind to none as to those to whom she has done no good.

392.--We should manage fortune like our health, enjoy it when it is good, be patient when it is bad, and never resort to strong remedies but in an extremity.

393.--Awkwardness sometimes disappears in the camp, never in the court.

394.--A man is often more clever than one other, but not than all others.

[“Singuli decipere ac decipi possunt, nemo omnes, omnes neminem fefellerunt.”--Pliny{ the Younger, PANEGYRICUS, LXII}.]

395.--We are often less unhappy at being deceived by one we loved, than on being deceived.

396.--We keep our first lover for a long time--if we do not get a second.

397.--We have not the courage to say generally that we have no faults, and that our enemies have no good qualities; but in fact we are not far from believing so.

398.--Of all our faults that which we most readily admit is idleness: we believe that it makes all virtues ineffectual, and that without utterly destroying, it at least suspends their operation.

399.--There is a kind of greatness which does not depend upon fortune: it is a certain manner what distinguishes us, and which seems to destine us for great things; it is the value we insensibly set upon ourselves; it is by this quality that we gain the deference of other men, and it is this which commonly raises us more above them, than birth, rank, or even merit itself.

400.--There may be talent without position, but there is no position without some kind of talent.

401.--Rank is to merit what dress is to a pretty woman.

402.--What we find the least of in flirtation is love.

403.--Fortune sometimes uses our faults to exalt us, and there are tiresome people whose deserts would be ill rewarded if we did not desire to purchase their absence.

404.--It appears that nature has hid at the bottom of our hearts talents and abilities unknown to us. It is only the passions that have the power of bringing them to light, and sometimes give us views more true and more perfect than art could possibly do.

405.--We reach quite inexperienced the different stages of life, and often, in spite of the number of our years, we lack experience.

[“To most men experience is like the stern lights of a ship which illumine only the track it has passed.”-- Coleridge.]

406.--Flirts make it a point of honour to be jealous of their lovers, to conceal their envy of other women.

407.--It may well be that those who have trapped us by their tricks do not seem to us so foolish as we seem to ourselves when trapped by the tricks of others.

408.--The most dangerous folly of old persons who have been loveable is to forget that they are no longer so.

[“Every woman who is not absolutely ugly thinks herself handsome. The suspicion of age no woman, let her be ever so old, forgives.”-- Lord Chesterfield, LETTER 129.]

409.--We should often be ashamed of our very best actions if the world only saw the motives which caused them.

410.--The greatest effort of friendship is not to show our faults to a friend, but to show him his own.

4ll.--We have few faults which are not far more excusable than the means we adopt to hide them.

412.--Whatever disgrace we may have deserved, it is almost always in our power to re-establish our cha- racter.

[“This is hardly a period at which the most irregular character may not be redeemed. The mistakes of one sin find a retreat in patriotism, those of the other in devotion.” -Junius, LETTER TO THE KING.]

413.--A man cannot please long who has only one kind of wit.

[According to Segrais this maxim was a hit at Racine and Boileau, who, despising ordinary conversation, talked incessantly of literature; but there is some doubt as to Segrais' statement.--Aim?Martin.]

414.--Idiots and lunatics see only their own wit.

415.--Wit sometimes enables us to act rudely with impunity.

416.--The vivacity which increases in old age is not far removed from folly.

[“How ill {white} hairs become {a} fool and jester.”-- Shakespeare{, King Henry IV, Part II, Act. V, Scene V, King}.

“Can age itself forget that you are now in the last act of life? Can grey hairs make folly venerable, and is there no period to be reserved for meditation or retirement.”-- Junius, TO THE DUKE OF BEDFORD, 19th Sept. 1769.]

417.--In love the quickest is always the best cure.

418.--Young women who do not want to appear flirts, and old men who do not want to appear ridi- culous, should not talk of love as a matter wherein they can have any interest.

419.--We may seem great in a post beneath our capacity, but we oftener seem little in a post above it.

420.--We often believe we have constancy in mis- fortune when we have nothing but debasement, and we suffer misfortunes without regarding them as cowards who let themselves be killed from fear of defending themselves.

421.--Conceit causes more conversation than wit.

422.--All passions make us commit some faults, love alone makes us ridiculous.

[“In love we all are fools alike.”--Gay{, THE BEGGAR'S OPERA, (1728), Act III, Scene I, Lucy}.]

423.--Few know how to be old.

424.--We often credit ourselves with vices the reverse of what we have, thus when weak we boast of our obstinacy.

425.--Penetration has a spice of divination in it which tickles our vanity more than any other quality of the mind.

426.--The charm of novelty and old custom, how- ever opposite to each other, equally blind us to the faults of our friends.

[“Two things the most opposite blind us equally, custom and novelty.”-La Bruyie, DES JUDGEMENTS.]

427.--Most friends sicken us of friendship, most devotees of devotion.

428.--We easily forgive in our friends those faults we do not perceive.

429.--Women who love, pardon more readily great indiscretions than little infidelities.

430.--In the old age of love as in life we still sur- vive for the evils, though no longer for the pleasures.

["The youth of friendship is better than its old age."-- Hazlitt's CHARACTERISTICS, 229.]

431.--Nothing prevents our being unaffected so much as our desire to seem so.

432.--To praise good actions heartily is in some measure to take part in them.

433.--The most certain sign of being born with great qualities is to be born without envy.

["Nemo alienae virtuti invidet qui satis confidet suae." - Cicero IN MARC ANT.]

434.--When our friends have deceived us we owe them but indifference to the tokens of their friend- ship, yet for their misfortunes we always owe them pity.

435.--Luck and temper rule the world.

436.--It is far easier to know men than to know man.

437.--We should not judge of a man's merit by his great abilities, but by the use he makes of them.

438.--There is a certain lively gratitude which not only releases us from benefits received, but which also, by making a return to our friends as payment, renders them indebted to us.

["And understood not that a grateful mind, By owing owes not, but is at once Indebted and discharged." Milton. PARADISE LOST.]

439.--We should earnestly desire but few things if we clearly knew what we desired.

440.--The cause why the majority of women are so little given to friendship is, that it is insipid after having felt love.

[“Those who have experienced a great passion neglect friendship, and those who have united themselves to friend- ship have nought to do with love.”--La Bruye. DU COEUR.]

441.--As in friendship so in love, we are often hap- pier from ignorance than from knowledge.

442.--We try to make a virtue of vices we are loth to correct.

443.--The most violent passions give some respite, but vanity always disturbs us.

444.--Old fools are more foolish than young fools.

[“MALVOLIO. Infirmity{,} that decays the wise{,} doth eve{r} make the better fool. CLOWN. God send you, sir, a speedy infirmity{,} for the better increasing of your folly.”--Shakespeare. TWELFTH NIGHT{, Act I, Scene V}.]

445.--Weakness is more hostile to virtue than vice.

446.--What makes the grief of shame and jealousy so acute is that vanity cannot aid us in enduring them.

447.--Propriety is the least of all laws, but the most obeyed.

[Honour has its supreme laws, to which education is bound to conform....Those things which honour forbids are more rigorously forbidden when the laws do not concur in the prohibition, and those it commands are more strongly insisted upon when they happen not to be commanded by law.--Montesquieu, {THE SPIRIT OF LAWS, }b. 4, c. ii.]

448.--A well-trained mind has less difficulty in sub- mitting to than in guiding an ill-trained mind.

449.--When fortune surprises us by giving us some great office without having gradually led us to expect it, or without having raised our hopes, it is well nigh impossible to occupy it well, and to appear worthy to fill it.

450.--Our pride is often increased by what we retrench from our other faults.

["The loss of sensual pleasures was supplied and com- pensated by spiritual pride."--Gibbon. DECLINE AND FALL, chap. xv.]

451.--No fools so wearisome as those who have some wit.

452.--No one believes that in every respect he is behind the man he considers the ablest in the world.

453.--In great matters we should not try so much to create opportunities as to utilise those that offer themselves.

[Yet Lord Bacon says "A wise man will make more opportunities than he finds."--Essays, {(1625), "Of Ceremonies and Respects"}]

454.--There are few occasions when we should make a bad bargain by giving up the good on condition that no ill was said of us.

455.--However disposed the world may be to judge wrongly, it far oftener favours false merit than does justice to true.

456.--Sometimes we meet a fool with wit, never one with discretion.

457.--We should gain more by letting the world see what we are than by trying to seem what we are not.

458.--Our enemies come nearer the truth in the opinions they form of us than we do in our opinion of ourselves.

459.--There are many remedies to cure love, yet none are infallible.

460.--It would be well for us if we knew all our passions make us do.

461.--Age is a tyrant who forbids at the penalty of life all the pleasures of youth.

462.--The same pride which makes us blame faults from which we believe ourselves free causes us to despise the good qualities we have not.

463.--There is often more pride than goodness in our grief for our enemies' miseries; it is to show how superior we are to them, that we bestow on them the sign of our compassion.

464.--There exists an excess of good and evil which surpasses our comprehension.

465.--Innocence is most fortunate if it finds the same protection as crime.

466.--Of all the violent passions the one that becomes a woman best is love.

467.--Vanity makes us sin more against our taste than reason.

468.--Some bad qualities form great talents.

469.--We never desire earnestly what we desire in reason.

470.--All our qualities are uncertain and doubtful, both the good as well as the bad, and nearly all are creatures of opportunities.

471.--In their first passion women love their lovers, in all the others they love love.

In her first passion woman loves her lover, In all her others what she loves is love.” {--Lord Byron, }Don Juan, Canto iii., stanza 3. “We truly love once, the first time; the subsequent pas- sions are more or less involuntary.” La Bruye: DU COEUR.]

472.--Pride as the other passions has its follies. We are ashamed to own we are jealous, and yet we plume ourselves in having been and being able to be so.

473.--However rare true love is, true friendship is rarer.

[“It is more common to see perfect love than real friend-ship.”--La Bruye. DU COEUR.]

474.--There are few women whose charm survives their beauty.

475.--The desire to be pitied or to be admired often forms the greater part of our confidence.

476.--Our envy always lasts longer than the happi- ness of those we envy.

477.--The same firmness that enables us to resist love enables us to make our resistance durable and lasting. So weak persons who are always excited by passions are seldom really possessed of any.

478.--Fancy does not enable us to invent so many different contradictions as there are by nature in every heart.

479.--It is only people who possess firmness who can possess true gentleness. In those who appear gentle it is generally only weakness, which is readily converted into harshness.

480.--Timidity is a fault which is dangerous to blame in those we desire to cure of it.

481.--Nothing is rarer than true good nature, those who think they have it are generally only pliant or weak.

482.--The mind attaches itself by idleness and habit to whatever is easy or pleasant. This habit always places bounds to our knowledge, and no one has ever yet taken the pains to enlarge and expand his mind to the full extent of its capacities.

483.--Usually we are more satirical from vanity than malice.

484.--When the heart is still disturbed by the relics of a passion it is proner to take up a new one than when wholly cured.

485.--Those who have had great passions often find all their lives made miserable in being cured of them.

486.--More persons exist without self-love than without envy.

[“I do not believe that there is a human creature in his senses arrived at maturity, that at some time or other has not been carried away by this passion (envy) in good earnest, and yet I never met with any who dared own he was guilty of it, but in jest.”--Mandeville: FABLE OF THE BEES; Remark N.]

487.--We have more idleness in the mind than in the body.

488.--The calm or disturbance of our mind does not depend so much on what we regard as the more important things of life, as in a judicious or injudicious arrangement of the little things of daily occurrence.

489.--However wicked men may be, they do not dare openly to appear the enemies of virtue, and when they desire to persecute her they either pretend to believe her false or attribute crimes to her.

490.--We often go from love to ambition, but we never return from ambition to love.

Men commence by love, finish by ambition, and do not find a quieter seat while they remain there.”--La Bruye: DU COEUR.]

491.--Extreme avarice is nearly always mistaken, there is no passion which is oftener further away from its mark, nor upon which the present has so much power to the prejudice of the future.

492.--Avarice often produces opposite results: there are an infinite number of persons who sacrifice their property to doubtful and distant expectations, others mistake great future advantages for small present interests.

[AIM?MARTIN says, “The author here confuses greedi- ness, the desire and avarice--passions which probably have a common origin, but produce different results. The greedy man is nearly always desirous to possess, and often foregoes great future advantages for small present interests. The avaricious man, on the other hand, mistakes present advantages for the great expectations of the future. Both desire to possess and enjoy. But the miser possesses and enjoys nothing but the pleasure of possessing; he risks nothing, gives nothing, hopes nothing, his life is centred in his strong box, beyond that he has no want.”]

493.--It appears that men do not find they have enough faults, as they increase the number by certain peculiar qualities that they affect to assume, and which they cultivate with so great assiduity that at length they become natural faults, which they can no longer correct.

494.--What makes us see that men know their faults better than we imagine, is that they are never wrong when they speak of their conduct; the same self-love that usually blinds them enlightens them, and gives them such true views as to make them suppress or disguise the smallest thing that might be censured.

495.--Young men entering life should be either shy or bold; a solemn and sedate manner usually de- generates into impertinence.

496.--Quarrels would not last long if the fault was only on one side.

497.--It is valueless to a woman to be young unless pretty, or to be pretty unless young.

498.--Some persons are so frivolous and fickle that they are as far removed from real defects as from substantial qualities.

499.--We do not usually reckon a woman's first flirtation until she has had a second.

500.--Some people are so self-occupied that when in love they find a mode by which to be engrossed with the passion without being so with the person they love.

501.--Love, though so very agreeable, pleases more by its ways than by itself.

502.--A little wit with good sense bores less in the long run than much wit with ill nature.

503.--Jealousy is the worst of all evils, yet the one that is least pitied by those who cause it.

504.--Thus having treated of the hollowness of so many apparent virtues, it is but just to say something on the hollowness of the contempt for death. I allude to that contempt of death which the heathen boasted they derived from their unaided understanding, with- out the hope of a future state. There is a difference between meeting death with courage and despising it. The first is common enough, the last I think always feigned. Yet everything that could be has been written to persuade us that death is no evil, and the weakest of men, equally with the bravest, have given many noble examples on which to found such an opinion, still I do not think that any man of good sense has ever yet believed in it. And the pains we take to persuade others as well as ourselves amply show that the task is far from easy. For many reasons we may be disgusted with life, but for none may we despise it. Not even those who commit suicide regard it as a light matter, and are as much alarmed and startled as the rest of the world if death meets them in a dif- ferent way than the one they have selected. The differ- ence we observe in the courage of so great a number of brave men, is from meeting death in a way different from what they imagined, when it shows itself nearer at one time than at another. Thus it ultimately happens that having despised death when they were ignorant of it, they dread it when they become acquainted with it. If we could avoid seeing it with all its surround- ings, we might perhaps believe that it was not the greatest of evils. The wisest and bravest are those who take the best means to avoid reflecting on it, as every man who sees it in its real light regards it as dreadful. The necessity of dying created all the con- stancy of philosophers. They thought it but right to go with a good grace when they could not avoid going, and being unable to prolong their lives indefinitely, nothing remained but to build an immortal reputation, and to save from the general wreck all that could be saved. To put a good face upon it, let it suffice, not to say all that we think to ourselves, but rely more on our nature than on our fallible reason, which might make us think we could approach death with indif- ference. The glory of dying with courage, the hope of being regretted, the desire to leave behind us a good reputation, the assurance of being enfranchised from the miseries of life and being no longer depend- ent on the wiles of fortune, are resources which should not be passed over. But we must not regard them as infallible. They should affect us in the same proportion as a single shelter affects those who in war storm a fortress. At a distance they think it may afford cover, but when near they find it only a feeble protection. It is only deceiving ourselves to imagine that death, when near, will seem the same as at a distance, or that our feelings, which are merely weaknesses, are naturally so strong that they will not suffer in an attack of the rudest of trials. It is equally as absurd to try the effect of self-esteem and to think it will enable us to count as naught what will of necessity destroy it. And the mind in which we trust to find so many resources will be far too weak in the struggle to persuade us in the way we wish. For it is this which betrays us so frequently, and which, instead of filling us with contempt of death, serves but to show us all that is frightful and fearful. The most it can do for us is to persuade us to avert our gaze and fix it on other objects. Cato and Brutus each selected noble ones. A lackey sometime ago contented himself by dancing on the scaffold when he was about to be broken on the wheel. So however diverse the motives they but realize the same result. For the rest it is a fact that whatever difference there may be between the peer and the peasant, we have constantly seen both the one and the other meet death with the same composure. Still there is always this difference, that the contempt the peer shows for death is but the love of fame which hides death from his sight; in the peasant it is but the result of his limited vision that hides from him the extent of the evil, end leaves him free to reflect on other things.

THE FIRST SUPPLEMENT

[The following reflections are extracted from the first two editions of La Rochefoucauld, having been suppressed by the author in succeeding issues.]

I.--Self-love is the love OF self, and of all things FOR self. It makes men self-worshippers, and if for- tune permits them, causes them to tyrannize over others; it is never quiet when out of itself, and only rests upon other subjects as a bee upon flowers, to extract from them its proper food. Nothing is so headstrong as its desires, nothing so well concealed as its designs, nothing so skilful as its management; its suppleness is beyond description; its changes surpass those of the metamorphoses, its refinements those of chemistry. We can neither plumb the depths nor pierce the shades of its recesses. Therein it is hidden from the most far-seeing eyes, therein it takes a thou- sand imperceptible folds. There it is often to itself invisible; it there conceives, there nourishes and rears, without being aware of it, numberless loves and hatreds, some so monstrous that when they are brought to light it disowns them, and cannot resolve to avow them. In the night which covers it are born the ridiculous persuasions it has of itself, thence come its errors, its ignorance, its silly mistakes; thence it is led to believe that its passions which sleep are dead, and to think that it has lost all appetite for that of which it is sated. But this thick darkness which con- ceals it from itself does not hinder it from seeing that perfectly which is out of itself; and in this it re- sembles our eyes which behold all, and yet cannot set their own forms. In fact, in great concerns and im- portant matters when the violence of its desires sum- mons all its attention, it sees, feels, hears, imagines, suspects, penetrates, divines all: so that we might think that each of its passions had a magic power proper to it. Nothing is so close and strong as its attachments, which, in sight of the extreme misfor- tunes which threaten it, it vainly attempts to break. Yet sometimes it effects that without trouble and quickly, which it failed to do with its whole power and in the course of years, whence we may fairly con- clude that it is by itself that its desires are inflamed, rather than by the beauty and merit of its objects, that its own taste embellishes and heightens them; that it is itself the game it pursues, and that it follows eagerly when it runs after that upon which itself is eager. It is made up of contraries. It is imperious and obedient, sincere and false, piteous and cruel, timid and bold. It has different desires according to the diversity of temperaments, which turn and fix it some- times upon riches, sometimes on pleasures. It changes according to our age, our fortunes, and our hopes; it is quite indifferent whether it has many or one, because it can split itself into many portions, and unite in one as it pleases. It is inconstant, and besides the changes which arise from strange causes it has an infinity born of itself, and of its own substance. It is inconstant through inconstancy, of lightness, love, novelty, lassitude and distaste. It is capricious, and one sees it sometimes work with intense eager- ness and with incredible labour to obtain things of little use to it which are even hurtful, but which it pursues because it wishes for them. It is silly, and often throws its whole application on the utmost frivolities. It finds all its pleasure in the dullest matters, and places its pride in the most contemptible. It is seen in all states of life, and in all conditions; it lives everywhere and upon everything; it subsists on nothing; it accommodates itself either to things or to the want of them; it goes over to those who are at war with it, enters into their designs, and, this is wonderful, it, with them, hates even itself; it conspires for its own loss, it works towards its own ruin--in fact, caring only to exist, and providing that it may BE, it will be its own enemy! We must therefore not be surprised if it is sometimes united to the rudest austerity, and if it enters so boldly into partnership to destroy her, because when it is rooted out in one place it re-esta- blishes itself in another. When it fancies that it abandons its pleasure it merely changes or suspends its enjoyment. When even it is conquered in its full flight, we find that it triumphs in its own defeat. Here then is the picture of self-love whereof the whole of our life is but one long agitation. The sea is its living image; and in the flux and reflux of its con- tinuous waves there is a faithful expression of the stormy succession of its thoughts and of its eternal motion. (Edition of 1665, No. 1.)

II.--Passions are only the different degrees of the heat or coldness of the blood. (1665, No. 13.)

III.--Moderation in good fortune is but apprehen- sion of the shame which follows upon haughtiness, or a fear of losing what we have. (1665, No. 18.)

IV.--Moderation is like temperance in eating; we could eat more but we fear to make ourselves ill. (1665, No. 21.)

V.--Everybody finds that to abuse in another which he finds worthy of abuse in himself. (1665, No. 33.)

VI.--Pride, as if tired of its artifices and its different metamorphoses, after having solely filled the divers parts of the comedy of life, exhibits itself with its natural face, and is discovered by haughtiness; so much so that we may truly say that haughtiness is but the flash and open declaration of pride. (1665, No. 37.)

VII.--One kind of happiness is to know exactly at what point to be miserable. (1665, No. 53.)

VIII.--When we do not find peace of mind (REPOS) in ourselves it is useless to seek it elsewhere. (1665, No. 53.)

IX.--One should be able to answer for one's fortune, so as to be able to answer for what we shall do. (1665, No. 70.)

X.--Love is to the soul of him who loves, what the soul is to the body which it animates. (1665, No. 77.)

XI.--As one is never at liberty to love or to cease from loving, the lover cannot with justice complain of the inconstancy of his mistress, nor she of the fickleness of her lover. (1665, No. 81.)

XII.--Justice in those judges who are moderate is but a love of their place. (1665, No. 89.)

XIII.--When we are tired of loving we are quite content if our mistress should become faithless, to loose us from our fidelity. (1665, No. 85.)

XIV.--The first impulse of joy which we feel at the happiness of our friends arises neither from our natural goodness nor from friendship; it is the result of self-love, which flatters us with being lucky in our own turn, or in reaping something from the good fortune of our friends. (1665, No. 97.)

XV.--In the adversity of our best friends we always find something which is not wholly displeasing to us. (1665, No. 99.)

[This gave occasion to Swift's celebrated “Verses on his own Death.” The four first are quoted opposite the title, then follow these lines:-- “This maxim more than all the rest, Is thought too base for human breast; In all distresses of our friends, We first consult our private ends; While nature kindly bent to ease us, Points out some circumstance to please us.”

See also Chesterfield's defence of this in his 129th letter; “they who know the deception and wickedness of the human heart will not be either romantic or blind enough to deny what Rochefoucauld and Swift have affirmed as a general truth.”]

XVI.--How shall we hope that another person will keep our secret if we do not keep it ourselves. (1665, No. 100.)

XVII.--As if it was not sufficient that self-love should have the power to change itself, it has added that of changing other objects, and this it does in a very astonishing manner; for not only does it so well disguise them that it is itself deceived, but it even changes the state and nature of things. Thus, when a female is adverse to us, and she turns her hate and persecution against us, self-love pronounces on her actions with all the severity of justice; it exaggerates the faults till they are enormous, and looks at her good qualities in so disadvan- tageous a light that they become more displeasing than her faults. If however the same female becomes favourable to us, or certain of our interests reconcile her to us, our sole self interest gives her back the lustre which our hatred deprived her of. The bad qualities become effaced, the good ones appear with a redoubled advantage; we even summon all our indulgence to justify the war she has made upon us. Now although all passions prove this truth, that of love exhibits it most clearly; for we may see a lover moved with rage by the neglect or the infidelity of her whom he loves, and meditating the utmost vengeance that his passion can inspire. Nevertheless as soon as the sight of his beloved has calmed the fury of his movements, his passion holds that beauty innocent; he only accuses himself, he condemns his condemnations, and by the miraculous power of self- love, he whitens the blackest actions of his mistress, and takes from her all crime to lay it on himself.

{No date or number is given for this maxim}

XVIII.--There are none who press so heavily on others as the lazy ones, when they have satisfied their idleness, and wish to appear industrious. (1666, No. 91.)

XIX.--The blindness of men is the most dangerous effect of their pride; it seems to nourish and augment it, it deprives us of knowledge of remedies which can solace our miseries and can cure our faults. (1665, No. 102.)

XX.--One has never less reason than when one despairs of finding it in others. (1665, No. 103.)

XXI.--Philosophers, and Seneca above all, have not diminished crimes by their precepts; they have only used them in the building up of pride. (1665, No. 105.)

XXII.--It is a proof of little friendship not to per- ceive the growing coolness of that of our friends. (1666, No. 97.)

XXIII.--The most wise may be so in indifferent and ordinary matters, but they are seldom so in their most serious affairs. (1665, No. 132.)

XXIV.--The most subtle folly grows out of the most subtle wisdom. (1665, No. 134.)

XXV.--Sobriety is the love of health, or an in- capacity to eat much. (l665, No. 135.)

XXVI.--We never forget things so well as when we are tired of talking of them. (1665, No. 144.)

XXVII.--The praise bestowed upon us is at least useful in rooting us in the practice of virtue. (1665, No. 155.)

XXVIII.--Self-love takes care to prevent him whom we flatter from being him who most flatters us. (1665, No. 157.)

XXIX.--Men only blame vice and praise virtue from interest. (1665, No. 151.)

XXX.--We make no difference in the kinds of anger, although there is that which is light and almost inno- cent, which arises from warmth of complexion, tem- perament, and another very criminal, which is, to speak properly, the fury of pride. (1665, No. 159.)

XXXI.--Great souls are not those who have fewer passions and more virtues than the common, but those only who have greater designs. (1665, No. 161.)

XXXII.--Kings do with men as with pieces of money; they make them bear what value they will, and one is forced to receive them according to their currency value, and not at their true worth. (1665, No. 165.)

[See Burns{, FOR A' THAT AN A' THAT}-- “The rank is but the guinea's stamp, {The} man's {the gowd} for a' that.” Also Farquhar and other parallel passages pointed out in FAMILIAR WORDS.]

XXXIII.--Natural ferocity makes fewer people cruel than self-love. (1665, No. 174.)

XXXIV.--One may say of all our virtues as an Italian poet says of the propriety of women, that it is often merely the art of appearing chaste. (1665, No. 176.)

XXXV.--There are crimes which become innocent and even glorious by their brilliancy,* their number, or their excess; thus it happens that public robbery is called financial skill, and the unjust capture of pro- vinces is called a conquest. (1665, No. 192.)

*<Some crimes may be excused by their brilliancy, such as those of Jael, of Deborah, of Brutus, and of Charlotte Corday--further than this the maxim is satire.>

XXXVI.--One never finds in man good or evil in excess. (1665, No. 201.)

XXXVII.--Those who are incapable of committing great crimes do not easily suspect others. (1665, No. {2}08.)

{The text incorrectly numbers this maxim as 508. It is 208.}

XXXVIII.--The pomp of funerals concerns rather the vanity of the living, than the honour of the dead. (1665, No. 213.)

XXXIX.--Whatever variety and change appears in the world, we may remark a secret chain, and a regu- lated order of all time by Providence, which makes everything follow in due rank and fall into its de- stined course. (1665, No. 225.)

XL.--Intrepidity should sustain the heart in con- spiracies in place of valour which alone furnishes all the firmness which is necessary for the perils of war. (1665, No. 231.)

XLI.--Those who wish to define victory by her birth will be tempted to imitate the poets, and to call her the Daughter of Heaven, since they cannot find her origin on earth. Truly she is produced from an infinity of actions, which instead of wishing to beget her, only look to the particular interests of their masters, since all those who compose an army, in aiming at their own rise and glory, produce a good so great and general. (1665, No. 232.)

XLII.--That man who has never been in danger cannot answer for his courage. (1665, No. 236.)

XLIII.--We more often place bounds on our grati- tude than on our desires and our hopes. (1665, No. 241.)

XLIV.--Imitation is always unhappy, for all which is counterfeit displeases by the very things which charm us when they are original (NATURELLES). (1665, No. 245.)

XLV.--We do not regret the loss of our friends ac- cording to THEIR merits, but according to OUR wants, and the opinion with which we believed we had im- pressed them of our worth. (1665, No. 248.)

XLVI.--It is very hard to separate the general goodness spread all over the world from great clever- ness. (1665, No. 252.)

XLVII.--For us to be always good, others should believe that they cannot behave wickedly to us with impunity. (1665, No. 254.)

XLVIII.--A confidence in being able to please is often an infallible means of being displeasing. (1665, No. 256.)

XLIX.--The confidence we have in ourselves arises in a great measure from that that we have in others. (1665, No. 258.)

L.--There is a general revolution which changes the tastes of the mind as well as the fortunes of the world. (1665, No. 250.)

LI.--Truth is foundation and the reason of the per- fection of beauty, for of whatever stature a thing may be, it cannot be beautiful and perfect unless it be truly that she should be, and possess truly all that she should have (1665, No. 260.)

[Beauty is truth, truth beauty.{--John Keats, “Ode on a a Grecian Urn,” (1820), Stanza 5}]

LII.--There are fine things which are more bril- liant when unfinished than when finished too much. (1665, No. 262.)

LIII.--Magnanimity is a noble effort of pride which makes a man master of himself, to make him master of all things. (1665, No. 271.)

LIV.--Luxury and too refined a policy in states are a sure presage of their fall, because all parties looking after their own interest turn away from the public good. (1665, No. 282.)

LV.--Of all passions that which is least known to us is idleness; she is the most ardent and evil of all, although her violence may be insensible, and the evils she causes concealed; if we consider her power attentively we shall find that in all encounters she makes herself mistress of our sentiments, our in- terests, and our pleasures; like the (fabled) Remora, she can stop the greatest vessels, she is a hidden rock, more dangerous in the most important matters than sudden squalls and the most violent tempests. The repose of idleness is a magic charm which suddenly suspends the most ardent pursuits and the most obstinate resolutions. In fact to give a true notion of this passion we must add that idleness, like a beati- tude of the soul, consoles us for all losses and fills the vacancy of all our wants. (1665, No. 290.)

LVI.--We are very fond of reading others' characters, but we do not like to be read ourselves. (1665, No. 296.)

LVII.--What a tiresome malady is that which forces one to preserve your health by a severe regimen. (IBID, No. 298.)

LVIII.--It is much easier to take love when one is free, than to get rid of it after having taken it. (1665, No. 300.)

LIX.--Women for the most part surrender them- selves more from weakness than from passion. Whence it is that bold and pushing men succeed better than others, although they are not so loveable. (1665, No. 301.)

LX.--Not to love is in love, an infallible means of being beloved. (1665, No. 302.)

LXI.--The sincerity which lovers and mistresses ask that both should know when they cease to love each other, arises much less from a wish to be warned of the cessation of love, than from a desire to be assured that they are beloved although no one denies it. (1665, No. 303.)

LXII.--The most just comparison of love is that of a fever, and we have no power over either, as to its violence or its duration. (1665, No. 305.)

LXIII.--The greatest skill of the least skilful is to know how to submit to the direction of another. (1665, No. 309.)

LXIV.--We always fear to see those whom we love when we have been flirting with others. (16{74}, No. 372.)

LXV.--We ought to console ourselves for our faults when we have strength enough to own them. (16{74}, No. 375.)

{The date of the previous two maxims is incorrectly cited as 1665 in the text. I found this date immediately suspect because the translators' introduction states that the 1665 edition only had 316 maxims. In fact, the two maxims only appeared in the fourth of the first five editions (1674).}

SECOND SUPPLEMENT.

REFLECTIONS, EXTRACTED FROM MS. LETTERS IN THE ROYAL LIBRARY.*

*<A LA BIBLIOTHEQUE DU ROI, it is difficult at present (June 1871) to assign a name to the magnificent collection of books in Paris, the property of the nation.>

LXVI.--Interest is the soul of self-love, in as much as when the body deprived of its soul is without sight, feeling or knowledge, without thought or movement, so self-love, riven so to speak from its interest, neither sees, nor hears, nor smells, nor moves; thus it is that the same man who will run over land and sea for his own interest becomes suddenly paralyzed when engaged for that of others; from this arises that sudden dulness and, as it were, death, with which we afflict those to whom we speak of our own matters; from this also their sudden resurrection when in our narrative we relate something concerning them; from this we find in our conversations and business that a man becomes dull or bright just as his own interest is near to him or distant from him. (LETTER TO MADAME DE SABL? MS., FOL. 211.)

LXVII.--Why we cry out so much against maxims which lay bare the heart of man, is because we fear that our own heart shall be laid bare. (MAXIM 103, MS., fol. 310.*)

*<The reader will recognise in these extracts portions of the Maxims previously given, sometimes the author has care- fully polished them; at other times the words are identical. Our numbers will indicate where they are to be found in the foregoing collection.>

LXVIII.--Hope and fear are inseparable. (TO MADAME DE SABL? MS., FOL. 222, MAX. 168.)

LXIX.--It is a common thing to hazard life to escape dishonour; but, when this is done, the actor takes very little pain to make the enterprise succeed in which he is engaged, and certain it is that they who hazard their lives to take a city or to conquer a pro- vince are better officers, have more merit, and wider and more useful, views than they who merely expose themselves to vindicate their honour; it is very com- mon to find people of the latter class, very rare to find those of the former. (LETTER TO M. ESPRIT, MS., FOL. 173, MAX. 219.)

LXX.--The taste changes, but the will remains the same. (TO MADAME DE SABL? FOL. 223, MAX. 252.)

LXXI.--The power which women whom we love have over us is greater than that which we have over ourselves. (TO THE SAME, MS., FOL. 211, MAX. 259)

LXXII.--That which makes us believe so easily that others have defects is that we all so easily believe what we wish. (TO THE SAME, MS., FOL. 223, MAX. 397.)

LXXIII.--I am perfectly aware that good sense and fine wit are tedious to every age, but tastes are not always the same, and what is good at one time will not seem so at another. This makes me think that few persons know how to be old. (TO THE SAME, FOL. 202, MAX. 423.)

LXXIV.--God has permitted, to punish man for his original sin, that he should be so fond of his self-love, that he should be tormented by it in all the actions of his life. (MS., FOL. 310, MAX. 494.)

LXXV.--And so far it seems to me the philosophy of a lacquey can go; I believe that all gaity in that state of life is very doubtful indeed. (TO MADAME DE SABL? FOL. 161, MAX. 504.)

[In the maxim cited the author relates how a footman about to be broken on the wheel danced on the scaffold. He seems to think that in his day the life of such servants was so miserable that their merriment was very doubtful.]

THIRD SUPPLEMENT

[The fifty following Maxims are taken from the Sixth Edition of the DE LA ROCHEFOUCAULD, published by Claude Barbin, in 1693, more than twelve years after the death of the author (17th May, 1680). The reader will find some repetitions, but also some very valuable maxims.]

LXXVI.--Many persons wish to be devout; but no one wishes to be humble.

LXXVII.--The labour of the body frees us from the pains of the mind, and thus makes the poor happy.

LXXVIII.--True penitential sorrows (mortifica- tions) are those which are not known, vanity renders the others easy enough.

LXXIX.--Humility is the altar upon which God wishes that we should offer him his sacrifices.

LXXX.--Few things are needed to make a wise man happy; nothing can make a fool content; that is why most men are miserable.

LXXXI.--We trouble ourselves less to become happy, than to make others believe we are so.

LXXXII.--It is more easy to extinguish the first desire than to satisfy those which follow.

LXXXIII.--Wisdom is to the soul what health is to the body.

LXXXIV.--The great ones of the earth can neither command health of body nor repose of mind, and they buy always at too dear a price the good they can acquire.

LXXXV.--Before strongly desiring anything we should examine what happiness he has who possesses it.

LXXXVI.--A true friend is the greatest of all goods, and that of which we think least of acquiring.

LXXXVII.--Lovers do not wish to see the faults of their mistresses until their enchantment is at an end.

LXXXVIII.--Prudence and love are not made for each other; in the ratio that love increases, prudence diminishes.

LXXXIX.--It is sometimes pleasing to a husband to have a jealous wife; he hears her always speaking of the beloved object.

XC.--How much is a woman to be pitied who is at the same time possessed of virtue and love!

XCI.--The wise man finds it better not to enter the encounter than to conquer.

[Somewhat similar to Goldsmith's sage-- “Who quits {a} world where strong temptations try, And since 'tis hard to co{mbat}, learns to fly.”]

XCII.--It is more necessary to study men than books.

["The proper study of mankind is man."--Pope {ESSAY ON MAN, (1733), EPISTLE II, line 2}.]

XCIII.--Good and evil ordinarily come to those who have most of one or the other.

XCIV.--The accent and character of one's native country dwells in the mind and heart as on the tongue. (REPITITION OF MAXIM 342.)

XCV.--The greater part of men have qualities which, like those of plants, are discovered by chance. (REPITITION OF MAXIM 344.)

XCVI.--A good woman is a hidden treasure; he who discovers her will do well not to boast about it. (SEE MAXIM 368.)

XCVII.--Most women do not weep for the loss of a lover to show that they have been loved so much as to show that they are worth being loved. (SEE MAXIM 362.)

XCVIII.--There are many virtuous women who are weary of the part they have played. (SEE MAXIM 367.)

XCIX.--If we think we love for love's sake we are much mistaken. (SEE MAXIM 374.)

C.--The restraint we lay upon ourselves to be con- stant, is not much better than an inconstancy. (SEE MAXIMS 369, 381.)

CI.--There are those who avoid our jealousy, of whom we ought to be jealous. (SEE MAXIM 359.)

CII.--Jealousy is always born with love, but does not always die with it. (SEE MAXIM 361.)

CIII.--When we love too much it is difficult to discover when we have ceased to be beloved.

CIV.--We know very well that we should not talk about our wives, but we do not remember that it is not so well to speak of ourselves. (SEE MAXIM 364.)

CV.--Chance makes us known to others and to our- selves. (SEE MAXIM 345.)

CVI.--We find very few people of good sense, ex- cept those who are of our own opinion. (SEE MAXIM 347.)

CVII.--We commonly praise the good hearts of those who admire us. (SEE MAXIM 356.)

CVIII.--Man only blames himself in order that he may be praised.

CIX.--Little minds are wounded by the smallest things. (SEE MAXIM 357.)

CX.--There are certain faults which placed in a good light please more than perfection itself. (SEE MAXIM 354.)

CXI.--That which makes us so bitter against those who do us a shrewd turn, is because they think them- selves more clever than we are. (SEE MAXIM 350.)

CXII.--We are always bored by those whom we bore. (SEE MAXIM 352.)

CXIII.--The harm that others do us is often less than that we do ourselves. (SEE MAXIM 363.)

CXIV.--It is never more difficult to speak well than when we are ashamed of being silent.

CXV.--Those faults are always pardonable that we have the courage to avow.

CXVI.--The greatest fault of penetration is not that it goes to the bottom of a matter--but beyond it. (SEE MAXIM 377.)

CXVII.--We give advice, but we cannot give the wisdom to profit by it. (SEE MAXIM 378.)

CXVIII.--When our merit declines, our taste de- clines also. (SEE MAXIM 379.)

CXIX.--Fortune discovers our vices and our vir- tues, as the light makes objects plain to the sight. (SEE MAXIM 380.)

CXX.--Our actions are like rhymed verse-ends (BOUTS-RIM) which everyone turns as he pleases. (SEE MAXIM 382.)

CXXI.--There is nothing more natural, nor more deceptive, than to believe that we are beloved.

CXXII.--We would rather see those to whom we have done a benefit, than those who have done us one.

CXXIII.--It is more difficult to hide the opinions we have than to feign those which we have not.

CXXIV.--Renewed friendships require more care than those that have never been broken.

CXXV.--A man to whom no one is pleasing is much more unhappy than one who pleases nobody.

REFLECTIONS ON VARIOUS SUBJECTS, BY THE DUKE DE LA ROCHEFOUCAULD

I. On Confidence.

Though sincerity and confidence have many points of resemblance, they have yet many points of difference.

Sincerity is an openness of heart, which shows us what we are, a love of truth, a dis- like to deception, a wish to compensate our faults and to lessen them by the merit of confessing them.

Confidence leaves us less liberty, its rules are stricter, it requires more prudence and reticence, and we are not always free to give it. It relates not only to ourselves, since our interests are often mixed up with those of others; it requires great delicacy not to expose our friends in exposing ourselves, not to draw upon their goodness to enhance the value of what we give.

Confidence always pleases those who receive it. It is a tribute we pay to their merit, a deposit we commit to their trust, a pledge which gives them a claim upon us, a kind of dependence to which we voluntarily submit. I do not wish from what I have said to depreciate confidence, so necessary to man. It is in society the link between acquaintance and friendship. I only wish to state its limits to make it true and real. I would that it was always sincere, always discreet, and that it had neither weakness nor interest. I know it is hard to place proper limits on being taken into all our friends' confidence, and taking them into all ours.

Most frequently we make confidants from vanity, a love of talking, a wish to win the confidence of others, and make an exchange of secrets.

Some may have a motive for confiding in us, towards whom we have no motive for confiding. With them we discharge the obligation in keeping their secrets and trusting them with small confidences.

Others whose fidelity we know trust nothing to us, but we confide in them by choice and inclina- tion.

We should hide from them nothing that concerns us, we should always show them with equal truth, our virtues and our vices, without exaggerating the one or diminishing the other. We should make it a rule never to have half confidences. They always embarrass those who give them, and dissatisfy those who receive them. They shed an uncertain light on what we want hidden, increase curiosity, entitling the recipients to know more, giving them leave to consider themselves free to talk of what they have guessed. It is far safer and more honest to tell nothing than to be silent when we have begun to tell. There are other rules to be observed in matters confided to us, all are important, to all prudence and trust are essential.

Everyone agrees that a secret should be kept intact, but everyone does not agree as to the nature and importance of secrecy. Too often we consult our-selves as to what we should say, what we should leave unsaid. There are few permanent secrets, and the scruple against revealing them will not last for ever.

With those friends whose truth we know we have the closest intimacy. They have always spoken unre- servedly to us, we should always do the same to them. They know our habits and connexions, and see too clearly not to perceive the slightest change. They may have elsewhere learnt what we have promised not to tell. It is not in our power to tell them what has been entrusted to us, though it might tend to their interest to know it. We feel as confident of them as of ourselves, and we are reduced to the hard fate of losing their friendship, which is dear to us, or of being faithless as regards a secret. This is doubtless the hardest test of fidelity, but it should not move an honest man; it is then that he can sacrifice himself to others. His first duty is to rigidly keep his trust in its entirety. He should not only control and guard his and his voice, but even his lighter talk, so that nothing be seen in his conversation or manner that could direct the curiosity of others towards that which he wishes to conceal.

We have often need of strength and prudence wherewith to oppose the exigencies of most of our friends who make a claim on our confidence, and seek to know all about us. We should never allow them to acquire this unexceptionable right. There are accidents and circumstances which do not fall in their cognizance; if they complain, we should endure their complaints and excuse ourselves with gentleness, but if they are still unreasonable, we should sacrifice their friendship to our duty, and choose between two inevitable evils, the one reparable, the other irre- parable.

II. On Difference of Character.

Although all the qualities of mind may be united in a great genius, yet there are some which are special and peculiar to him; his views are unlimited; he always acts uniformly and with the same activity; he sees distant objects as if present; he compre- hends and grasps the greatest, sees and notices the smallest matters; his thoughts are elevated, broad, just and intelligible. Nothing escapes his observation, and he often finds truth in spite of the obscurity that hides her from others.

A lofty mind always thinks nobly, it easily creates vivid, agreeable, and natural fancies, places them in their best light, clothes them with all appropriate adornments, studies others' tastes, and clears away from its own thoughts all that is useless and dis- agreeable.

A clever, pliant, winning mind knows how to avoid and overcome difficulties. Bending easily to what it wants, it understands the inclination and temper it is dealing with, and by managing their interests it advances and establishes its own.

A well regulated mind sees all things as they should be seen, appraises them at their proper value, turns them to its own advantage, and adheres firmly to its own opinions as it knows all their force and weight.

A difference exists between a working mind and a business-like mind. We can undertake business with- out turning it to our own interest. Some are clever only in what does not concern them, and the reverse in all that does. There are others again whose cleverness is limited to their own business, and who know how to turn everything to their own advantage.

It is possible to have a serious turn of mind, and yet to talk pleasantly and cheerfully. This class of mind is suited to all persons in all times of life. Young persons have usually a cheerful and satirical turn, untempered by seriousness, thus often making themselves disagreeable.

No part is easier to play than that of being always pleasant; and the applause we sometimes receive in censuring others is not worth being exposed to the chance of offending them when they are out of temper.

Satire is at once the most agreeable and most dan- gerous of mental qualities. It always pleases when it is refined, but we always fear those who use it too much, yet satire should be allowed when unmixed with spite, and when the person satirised can join in the satire.

It is unfortunate to have a satirical turn without affecting to be pleased or without loving to jest. It requires much adroitness to continue satirical with- out falling into one of these extremes.

Raillery is a kind of mirth which takes possession of the imagination, and shows every object in an absurd light; wit combines more or less softness or harshness.

There is a kind of refined and flattering raillery that only hits the faults that persons admit, which under- stands how to hide the praise it gives under the ap- pearance of blame, and shows the good while feigning a wish to hide it.

An acute mind and a cunning mind are very dis- similar. The first always pleases; it is unfettered, it perceives the most delicate and sees the most impercep- tible matters. A cunning spirit never goes straight, it endeavours to secure its object by byeways and short cuts. This conduct is soon found out, it always gives rise to distrust and never reaches greatness.

There is a difference between an ardent and a brilliant mind, a fiery spirit travels further and faster, while a brilliant mind is sparkling, attractive, accu- rate.

Gentleness of mind is an easy and accommodating manner which always pleases when not insipid.

A mind full of details devotes itself to the manage- ment and regulation of the smallest particulars it meets with. This distinction is usually limited to little matters, yet it is not absolutely incompatible with greatness, and when these two qualities are united in the same mind they raise it infinitely above others.

The expression "BEL ESPRIT" is much perverted, for all that one can say of the different kinds of mind meet together in the "BEL ESPRIT." Yet as the epithet is bestowed on an infinite number of bad poets and tedious authors, it is more often used to ridicule than to praise.

There are yet many other epithets for the mind which mean the same thing, the difference lies in the tone and manner of saying them, but as tones and manner cannot appear in writing I shall not go into distinctions I cannot explain. Custom explains this in saying that a man has wit, has much wit, that he is a great wit; there are tones and manners which make all the difference between phrases which seem all alike on paper, and yet express a different order of mind.

So we say that a man has only one kind of wit, that he has several, that he has every variety of wit.

One can be a fool with much wit, and one need not be a fool even with very little wit.

To have much mind is a doubtful expression. It may mean every class of mind that can be mentioned, it may mean none in particular. It may mean that he talks sensibly while he acts foolishly. We may have a mind, but a narrow one. A mind may be fitted for some things, not for others. We may have a large measure of mind fitted for nothing, and one is often inconvenienced with much mind; still of this kind of mind we may say that it is sometimes pleasing in society.

Though the gifts of the mind are infinite, they can, it seems to me, be thus classified.

There are some so beautiful that everyone can see and feel their beauty.

There are some lovely, it is true, but which are wearisome.

There are some which are lovely, which all the world admire, but without knowing why.

There are some so refined and delicate that few are capable even of remarking all their beauties.

There are others which, though imperfect, yet are produced with such skill, and sustained and managed with such sense and grace, that they even deserve to be admired.

III. On Taste.

Some persons have more wit than taste, others have more taste than wit. There is greater vanity and caprice in taste than in wit.

The word taste has different meanings, which it is easy to mistake. There is a difference between the taste which in certain objects has an attraction for us, and the taste that makes us understand and distinguish the qualities we judge by.

We may like a comedy without having a sufficiently fine and delicate taste to criticise it accurately. Some tastes lead us imperceptibly to objects, from which others carry us away by their force or intensity.

Some persons have bad taste in everything, others have bad taste only in some things, but a correct and good taste in matters within their capacity. Some have peculiar taste, which they know to be bad, but which they still follow. Some have a doubtful taste, and let chance decide, their indecision makes them change, and they are affected with pleasure or weari- ness on their friends' judgment. Others are always prejudiced, they are the slaves of their tastes, which they adhere to in everything. Some know what is good, and are horrified at what is not; their opinions are clear and true, and they find the reason for their taste in their mind and understanding.

Some have a species of instinct (the source of which they are ignorant of), and decide all questions that come before them by its aid, and always decide rightly.

These follow their taste more than their intelligence, because they do not permit their temper and self-love to prevail over their natural discernment. All they do is in harmony, all is in the same spirit. This harmony makes them decide correctly on matters, and form a correct estimate of their value. But speaking generally there are few who have a taste fixed and independent of that of their friends, they follow example and fashion which generally form the stand- ard of taste.

In all the diversities of taste that we discern, it is very rare and almost impossible to meet with that sort of good taste that knows how to set a price on the particular, and yet understands the right value that should be placed on all. Our knowledge is too limited, and that correct discernment of good qualities which goes to form a correct judgment is too seldom to be met with except in regard to matters that do not concern us.

As regards ourselves our taste has not this all- important discernment. Preoccupation, trouble, all that concern us, present it to us in another aspect. We do not see with the same eyes what does and what does not relate to us. Our taste is guided by the bent of our self-love and temper, which supplies us with new views which we adapt to an infinite number of changes and uncertainties. Our taste is no longer our own, we cease to control it, without our consent it changes, and the same objects appear to us in such divers aspects that ultimately we fail to per- ceive what we have seen and heard.

IV. On Society.

In speaking of society my plan is not to speak of friendship, for, though they have some connection, they are yet very different. The former has more in it of greatness and humility, and the greatest merit of the latter is to resemble the former.

For the present I shall speak of that particular kind of intercourse that gentlemen should have with each other. It would be idle to show how far society is essential to men: all seek for it, and all find it, but few adopt the method of making it pleasant and lasting.

Everyone seeks to find his pleasure and his advan- tage at the expense of others. We prefer ourselves always to those with whom we intend to live, and they almost always perceive the preference. It is this which disturbs and destroys society. We should discover a means to hide this love of selection since it is too ingrained in us to be in our power to destroy. We should make our pleasure that of other persons, to humour, never to wound their self-love.

The mind has a great part to do in so great a work, but it is not merely sufficient for us to guide it in the different courses it should hold.

The agreement we meet between minds would not keep society together for long if she was not governed and sustained by good sense, temper, and by the con- sideration which ought to exist between persons who have to live together.

It sometimes happens that persons opposite in tem- per and mind become united. They doubtless hold together for different reasons, which cannot last for long. Society may subsist between those who are our inferiors by birth or by personal qualities, but those who have these advantages should not abuse them. They should seldom let it be perceived that they serve to instruct others. They should let their con- duct show that they, too, have need to be guided and led by reason, and accommodate themselves as far as possible to the feeling and the interests of the others.

To make society pleasant, it is essential that each should retain his freedom of action. A man should not see himself, or he should see himself without dependence, and at the same time amuse himself. He should have the power of separating himself without that separation bringing any change on the society. He should have the power to pass by one and the other, if he does not wish to expose himself to occa- sional embarrassments; and he should remember that he is often bored when he believes he has not the power even to bore. He should share in what he believes to be the amusement of persons with whom he wishes to live, but he should not always be liable to the trouble of providing them.

Complaisance is essential in society, but it should have its limits, it becomes a slavery when it is extreme. We should so render a free consent, that in following the opinion of our friends they should believe that they follow ours.

We should readily excuse our friends when their faults are born with them, and they are less than their good qualities. We should often avoid to show what they have said, and what they have left unsaid. We should try to make them perceive their faults, so as to give them the merit of correcting them.

There is a kind of politeness which is necessary in the intercourse among gentlemen, it makes them comprehend badinage, and it keeps them from using and employing certain figures of speech, too rude and unrefined, which are often used thoughtlessly when we hold to our opinion with too much warmth.

The intercourse of gentlemen cannot subsist without a certain kind of confidence; this should be equal on both sides. Each should have an appearance of sincerity and of discretion which never causes the fear of anything imprudent being said.

There should be some variety in wit. Those who have only one kind of wit cannot please for long unless they can take different roads, and not both use the same talents, thus adding to the pleasure of society, and keeping the same harmony that different voices and different instruments should observe in music; and as it is detrimental to the quiet of society, that many persons should have the same interests, it is yet as necessary for it that their interests should not be different.

We should anticipate what can please our friends, find out how to be useful to them so as to exempt them from annoyance, and when we cannot avert evils, seem to participate in them, insensibly obliterate without attempting to destroy them at a blow, and place agreeable objects in their place, or at least such as will interest them. We should talk of subjects that concern them, but only so far as they like, and we should take great care where we draw the line. There is a species of politeness, and we may say a similar species of humanity, which does not enter too quickly into the recesses of the heart. It often takes pains to allow us to see all that our friends know, while they have still the advantage of not knowing to the full when we have penetrated the depth of the heart.

Thus the intercourse between gentlemen at once gives them familiarity and furnishes them with an infinite number of subjects on which to talk freely.

Few persons have sufficient tact and good sense fairly to appreciate many matters that are essential to maintain society. We desire to turn away at a certain point, but we do not want to be mixed up in everything, and we fear to know all kinds of truth.

As we should stand at a certain distance to view objects, so we should also stand at a distance to observe society; each has its proper point of view from which it should be regarded. It is quite right that it should not be looked at too closely, for there is hardly a man who in all matters allows himself to be seen as he really is.

V. On Conversation.

The reason why so few persons are agreeable in con- versation is that each thinks more of what he desires to say, than of what the others say, and that we make bad listeners when we want to speak.

Yet it is necessary to listen to those who talk, we should give them the time they want, and let them say even senseless things; never contradict or interrupt them; on the contrary, we should enter into their mind and taste, illustrate their meaning, praise anything they say that deserves praise, and let them see we praise more from our choice than from agreement with them.

To please others we should talk on subjects they like and that interest them, avoid disputes upon in- different matters, seldom ask questions, and never let them see that we pretend to be better informed than they are.

We should talk in a more or less serious manner, and upon more or less abstruse subjects, according to the temper and understanding of the persons we talk with, and readily give them the advantage of deciding without obliging them to answer when they are not anxious to talk.

After having in this way fulfilled the duties of politeness, we can speak our opinions to our listeners when we find an opportunity without a sign of presumption or opinionatedness. Above all things we should avoid often talking of ourselves and giving ourselves as an example; nothing is more tiresome than a man who quotes himself for everything.

We cannot give too great study to find out the manner and the capacity of those with whom we talk, so as to join in the conversation of those who have more than ourselves without hurting by this prefer- ence the wishes or interests of others.

Then we should modestly use all the modes above- mentioned to show our thoughts to them, and make them, if possible, believe that we take our ideas from them.

We should never say anything with an air of authority, nor show any superiority of mind. We should avoid far-fetched expressions, expressions hard or forced, and never let the words be grander than the matter.

It is not wrong to retain our opinions if they are reasonable, but we should yield to reason, wherever she appears and from whatever side she comes, she alone should govern our opinions, we should follow her without opposing the opinions of others, and without seeming to ignore what they say.

It is dangerous to seek to be always the leader of the conversation, and to push a good argument too hard, when we have found one. Civility often hides half its understanding, and when it meets with an opinionated man who defends the bad side, spares him the disgrace of giving way.

We are sure to displease when we speak too long and too often of one subject, and when we try to turn the conversation upon subjects that we think more instructive than others, we should enter indifferently upon every subject that is agreeable to others, stop- ping where they wish, and avoiding all they do not agree with.

Every kind of conversation, however witty it may be, is not equally fitted for all clever persons; we should select what is to their taste and suitable to their condition, their sex, their talents, and also choose the time to say it.

We should observe the place, the occasion, the temper in which we find the person who listens to us, for if there is much art in speaking to the purpose, there is no less in knowing when to be silent. There is an eloquent silence which serves to approve or to condemn, there is a silence of discretion and of respect. In a word, there is a tone, an air, a manner, which renders everything in conversation agreeable or dis- agreeable, refined or vulgar.

But it is given to few persons to keep this secret well. Those who lay down rules too often break them, and the safest we are able to give is to listen much, to speak little, and to say nothing that will ever give ground for regret.

VI. Falsehood.

We are false in different ways. There are some men who are false from wishing always to appear what they are not. There are some who have better faith, who are born false, who deceive themselves, and who never see themselves as they really are; to some is given a true understanding and a false taste, others have a false understanding and some correctness in taste; there are some who have not any falsity either in taste or mind. These last are very rare, for to speak generally, there is no one who has not some falseness in some corner of his mind or his taste.

What makes this falseness so universal, is that as our qualities are uncertain and confused, so too, are our tastes; we do not see things exactly as they are, we value them more or less than they are worth, and do not bring them into unison with ourselves in a manner which suits them or suits our condition or qualities.

This mistake gives rise to an infinite number of falsities in the taste and in the mind. Our self-love is flattered by all that presents itself to us under the guise of good.

But as there are many kinds of good which affect our vanity and our temper, so they are often followed from custom or advantage. We follow because the others follow, without considering that the same feeling ought not to be equally embarrassing to all kinds of persons, and that it should attach itself more or less firmly, according as persons agree more or less with those who follow them.

We dread still more to show falseness in taste than in mind. Gentleness should approve without preju- dice what deserves to be approved, follow what deserves to be followed, and take offence at nothing. But there should be great distinction and great accuracy. We should distinguish between what is good in the abstract and what is good for ourselves, and always follow in reason the natural inclination which carries us towards matters that please us.

If men only wished to excel by the help of their own talents, and in following their duty, there would be nothing false in their taste or in their conduct. They would show what they were, they would judge matters by their lights, and they would attract by their reason. There would be a discernment in their views, in their sentiments, their taste would be true, it would come to them direct, and not from others, they would follow from choice and not from habit or chance. If we are false in admiring what should not be admired, it is oftener from envy that we affix a value to qualities which are good in themselves, but which do not become us. A magistrate is false when he flatters himself he is brave, and that he will be able to be bold in certain cases. He should be as firm and stedfast in a plot which ought to be stifled without fear of being false, as he would be false and absurd in fighting a duel about it.

A woman may like science, but all sciences are not suitable for her, and the doctrines of certain sciences never become her, and when applied by her are always false.

We should allow reason and good sense to fix the value of things, they should determine our taste and give things the merit they deserve, and the im- portance it is fitting we should give them. But nearly all men are deceived in the price and in the value, and in these mistakes there is always a kind of falseness.

VII. On Air and Manner.

There is an air which belongs to the figure and talents of each individual; we always lose it when we abandon it to assume another.

We should try to find out what air is natural to us and never abandon it, but make it as perfect as we can. This is the reason that the majority of children please. It is because they are wrapt up in the air and manner nature has given them, and are ignorant of any other. They are changed and corrupted when they quit infancy, they think they should imitate what they see, and they are not altogether able to imitate it. In this imitation there is always something of falsity and uncertainty. They have nothing settled in their man- ner and opinions. Instead of being in reality what they want to appear, they seek to appear what they are not.

All men want to be different, and to be greater than they are; they seek for an air other than their own, and a mind different from what they possess; they take their style and manner at chance. They make experiments upon themselves without considering that what suits one person will not suit everyone, that there is no universal rule for taste or manners, and that there are no good copies.

Few men, nevertheless, can have unison in many matters without being a copy of each other, if each follow his natural turn of mind. But in general a person will not wholly follow it. He loves to imitate. We often imitate the same person without perceiving it, and we neglect our own good qualities for the good qualities of others, which generally do not suit us.

I do not pretend, from what I say, that each should so wrap himself up in himself as not to be able to follow example, or to add to his own, useful and serviceable habits, which nature has not given him. Arts and sciences may be proper for the greater part of those who are capable for them. Good manners and politeness are proper for all the world. But, yet acquired qualities should always have a certain agree- ment and a certain union with our own natural qualities, which they imperceptibly extend and in- crease. We are elevated to a rank and dignity above ourselves. We are often engaged in a new profession for which nature has not adapted us. All these con- ditions have each an air which belong to them, but which does not always agree with our natural manner. This change of our fortune often changes our air and our manners, and augments the air of dignity, which is always false when it is too marked, and when it is not united and amalgamated with that which nature has given us. We should unite and blend them to- gether, and thus render them such that they can never be separated.

We should not speak of all subjects in one tone and in the same manner. We do not march at the head of a regiment as we walk on a pro- menade; and we should use the same style in which we should naturally speak of different things in the same way, with the same difference as we should walk, but always naturally, and as is suitable, either at the head of a regiment or on a promenade. There are some who are not content to abandon the air and manner natural to them to assume those of the rank and dignities to which they have arrived. There are some who assume prematurely the air of the dignities and rank to which they aspire. How many lieutenant- generals assume to be marshals of France, how many barristers vainly repeat the style of the Chancellor and how many female citizens give themselves the airs of duchesses.

But what we are most often vexed at is that no one knows how to conform his air and manners with his appearance, nor his style and words with his thoughts and sentiments, that every one forgets himself and how far he is insensibly removed from the truth. Nearly every one falls into this fault in some way. No one has an ear sufficiently fine to mark perfectly this kind of cadence.

Thousands of people with good qualities are dis- pleasing; thousands pleasing with far less abilities, and why? Because the first wish to appear to be what they are not, the second are what they appear.

Some of the advantages or disadvantages that we have received from nature please in proportion as we know the air, the style, the manner, the senti- ments that coincide with our condition and our appearance, and displease in the proportion they are removed from that point.

###

www.ingramcontent.com/pod-product-compliance
Lightning Source LLC
Chambersburg PA
CBHW071054290526
45795CB00004B/1493